LIGHTHOUSES
of the
GREAT LAKES
Ontario, Erie, Huron, Michigan, and Superior

RAY JONES

Globe
Pequot

Essex, Connecticut

Globe Pequot

An imprint of Globe Pequot, the trade division of
The Rowman & Littlefield Publishing Group, Inc.
4501 Forbes Blvd., Ste. 200
Lanham, MD 20706
www.rowman.com

Distributed by NATIONAL BOOK NETWORK

British Library Cataloguing in Publication Information available

Library of Congress Cataloging-in-Publication Data

Names: Jones, Ray, 1948– author.
Title: Lighthouses of the Great Lakes : Ontario, Erie, Huron, Michigan, and
    Superior / Ray Jones.
Description: Essex, Connecticut : Globe Pequot, [2023] | Includes index.
Identifiers: LCCN 2022047921 (print) | LCCN 2022047922 (ebook) | ISBN
    9781493047307 (paper) | ISBN 9781493047314 (epub)
Subjects: LCSH: Lighthouses—Great Lakes (North America)—Guidebooks.
Classification: LCC VK1023.3 .J66 2023 (print) | L CC VK1023.3 (ebook) |
    DDC 386/.855/0977—dc23/eng/20221012
LC record available at https://lccn.loc.gov/2022047921
LC ebook record available at https://lccn.loc.gov/2022047922

♾️™ The paper used in this publication meets the minimum requirements of American National Standard for Information Sciences—Permanence of Paper for Printed Library Materials, ANSI/NISO Z39.48-1992.

Contents

PART THREE
ROMANTIC BEACONS OF
THE THUNDER LAKE: HURON

PART FOUR
ROMANTIC BEACONS OF
THE ALL-AMERICAN LAKE: MICHIGAN

PART FIVE
ROMANTIC BEACONS OF
THE LEVIATHAN LAKE: SUPERIOR

PART SIX
ROMANTIC BEACONS OF
THE IMPERIAL COAST

Introduction

Among the thousands of vessels that have been lost on the Great Lakes was the very first European-style trading ship to sail the lakes' wide, open waters. In 1679 the French explorer Sieur de La Salle and a party of fur traders built a 50-ton sailing ship, pushing her off into Lake Erie from a rough-hewn shipyard near where the City of Buffalo, New York, now stands. This was no crude, overbuilt canoe. Christened the *Griffin*, she was more than 60 feet long and had five cannons arrayed below the deck. La Salle and his fellow adventurers intended to make themselves rich by filling the *Griffin's* holds with muskrat and beaver pelts gathered by French trappers. The *Griffin* proved a worthy ship, weathering more than one fierce storm on the outbound leg of her maiden voyage to the far reaches of the Great Lakes.

Eventually, La Salle disembarked to continue his explorations (and discover the upper Mississippi River). As he watched the *Griffin* sail away eastward, La Salle was confident that the ship and her treasured cargo of furs would safely reach their destination. But neither the *Griffin* nor her crew would ever be heard from again. Probably, like so many other unlucky ships that came after, she was smashed to bits by a sudden, sharp autumn gale. Some believe that her rotting ribs lie near the Mississagi Straits Lighthouse on Lake Huron. If the lighthouse had been there to guide the *Griffin* when she sailed into the straits more than 300 years ago, perhaps commercial shipping on the Great Lakes would not have gotten off to such an unfortunate and ominous beginning.

America's Inland Seas

Ontario. Erie. Huron. Michigan. Superior. These are no ordinary lakes. First consider their size. A journey from Cleveland, Ohio, on the southern shore of Lake Erie, to Duluth, Minnesota, on the western reaches of Lake Superior, will cover more than 700 miles—and on this trip the traveler would not traverse the 307-mile length of Lake Michigan or the 193-mile length of Lake Ontario. The lakes are so large that they are easily recognized from space. They have been seen and identified by astronauts standing on the moon.

Taken together, the Great Lakes comprise by far the largest body of fresh water on the planet. They form what is quite literally an inland freshwater sea. As such, they invite comparison to the Earth's other great seas: the Red, the Black, the Baltic, the North, the Caspian, the Aral (actually much smaller than Lake Superior), and others. But the most interesting and instructive comparison may be with the world's most famous sea, the Mediterranean. Born in a desert, the Mediterranean was once an enormous, sandy basin with a mostly dry, sun-scorched floor. When Spain parted from the

African continent several million years ago, the Atlantic poured through the Strait of Gibraltar, also known as the "Gates of Hercules," and turned the desert into a sea. The Mediterranean retains some of the qualities of a sunny desert even today. It evaporates more water than it receives from its rivers. Thus, should the movements of the continents ever close the strait, the Mediterranean would eventually dry up and become once more a parched basin. In contrast, if some geological upheaval were suddenly to reverse the flow of the St. Lawrence River (and the upper Mississippi), the watery abundance of the Great Lakes would inundate the entire Midwest.

Unlike the Mediterranean, the Great Lakes were the product not of a desert environment but rather a frozen one. Four times during the last million years, heavy blankets of ice reached southward across the North American continent. After each advance, the ice retreated, leaving behind enormous lakes. The last of these ice ages, known to scientists as the Wisconsin Advance, ended about 10,000 years ago—in geological time, the blink of an eye. Relative to the age of the Earth, which is measured in billions of years, the lakes that we see today are very young indeed. And when their waters are torn by the storms that come whistling out of the center of the continent, they show their youthful temper.

Although they are unruly children by comparison, the lakes have more than a little in common with the much older and larger Mediterranean Sea. Both these mostly enclosed bodies of water are products of a geological revolution, and both have nurtured a revolution. The trade made possible by the readily navigable waters of the Mediterranean formed the economic basis of Greek culture, of the Roman Empire—indeed, of all Western civilization. Many centuries later the freighters scurrying back and forth through the Great Lakes would fuel another economic miracle: the American Industrial Renaissance. These changes, however—though most would call them beneficial to humanity—came at a heavy price.

As Ulysses and countless sailors of later eras would discover, those who sail the Earth's seas, whether they be salty or not, must be prepared for rough waters. The floor of the Mediterranean is a graveyard littered with the hulks of rotting ships. Similarly, the Great Lakes serve as a vast tomb for wrecked ships and hapless crews. At least 6,000 large vessels have found their final resting place at the bottom of the five big lakes.

The Great Lakes have always presented sailors with a special challenge. Because they are located near the center of one of the Earth's largest landmasses, the weather patterns that sweep across the lakes are quite different from—and often more violent than—those encountered on the open ocean. North America receives heavier snows than any other continent, so the lakes are the snowiest navigable bodies of water on the planet.

But potentially blinding snow squalls are only one of a lake sailor's many concerns. Storms driven by the sharp temperature differences over land and water can strike swiftly and with extraordinary intensity. Skies may clear again in a matter of minutes, or the heavy weather may go on for days. Since fresh water is lighter than salt water, wind-driven waves that batter the sides of ships tend to mount higher. The lakes' narrow widths and even narrower channels leave ships little room to maneuver. And there are countless ship-killing shoals and low, almost invisible headlands waiting to devour any vessel and crew that stray too far off course.

The lakes are so unpredictable and, at times, so dangerous that regular commercial shipping would be impossible without an extensive, well-planned network of navigational aids. Today the US and Canadian coast guards help guide ships through the lakes with an increasing array of high-tech direction-finding equipment, radio beacons, and radar. Thousands of buoys and channel lights now mark the lakes as well or better than any highway on land. One might almost think lake sailors should stow their charts and compasses and buy road maps. Not so! Most of the time—and always in a storm—lake sailors are on their own. They must rely on their eyes and their own good judgment to help them navigate safely. And on a dark night or in a gale, when captains or pilots are seen with binoculars in hand, they are most likely looking for the beacon of a lighthouse.

Lighting the Lakes

For as long as ships have sailed the seas, sailors nearing land have counted on shore lights to help them determine their positions, avoid dangerous obstacles, and find safe harbor. The earliest maritime peoples banked fires on hillsides to bring their ships home from the sea. Occasionally, port cities and towns lacking suitable high ground for this purpose erected towers and placed a lamp or built a small fire at the top.

No one can say for certain where the world's first true lighthouse was located, but the first that we know of served the Greco-Egyptian city of Alexandria. Soaring 450 feet into the sunny Mediterranean skies, it was also history's tallest lighthouse and the one with the longest service record. Built about 280 BC on an island called Pharos, inside Alexandria's bustling harbor, it stood for more than a thousand years before being toppled by an earthquake near the end of the first millennium AD. At night keepers lit a bright fire at the top of the huge tower to guide Phoenicians, Greeks, Carthaginians, Romans, and other mariners from all over the known world to this fabled and prosperous city. Most came to load up their ships with grain from the Nile Delta. The rich soil of the delta was so wondrously productive that its grains made possible the Roman Empire and fed soldiers and city dwellers all around the Mediterranean Basin. But the grain would never have reached market without the ships that carried it and the lighthouse that guided their captains to port.

Like the Mediterranean of Roman times, North America's inland seas are a heavily traveled commercial thoroughfare. Great Lakes freighters carry an endless variety of raw materials and finished products—iron ore to steel mills, metal parts to auto-assembly plants, oil and chemicals to refineries, grain from the prodigious farms of

the Midwest to hungry peoples all over the world. The Great Lakes have been a key driving force in the American and Canadian economies, and the long lake freighters and their brave crews have fueled that engine. But the prosperity brought by commerce has come at a high price: thousands of ships sunk and thousands of sailors drowned.

Yet the cost in vessels and lives would have been even higher if not for the lighthouses that ring each of the lakes. For more than a century, lake sailors have been guided by a linked chain of navigational lights extending for more than 1,000 miles, from the St. Lawrence River to Duluth. Many of the lights, such as the Charlotte–Genesee Light in Rochester, New York, and the Gibraltar Point Light in Toronto, Ontario, have shined out over the lake waters since the United States and Canada were very young nations. Most lake lighthouses are at least a century old, and all have played an essential role in the economic development and history of the United States and Canada.

Through dramatic photographs and narrative, this book tells the story of the most historically significant, scenic, and romantic lighthouses on all five of the Great Lakes. Travel information is included for those who wish to discover these architectural and historic treasures for themselves. Join us now as we follow a trail of lighthouses leading deep into the heart of a continent.

For more than a century, the Grand Marias Lighthouse (opposite page) has called mariners home from the dark waters of Lake Superior. Only 33 feet tall, this relatively small tower and it's bright fifth-order beacon have no doubt saved many lives. Dozens of other towers and beacons scattered throughout the Great Lakes have saved countless others. Of course, some they could not save.
LAYNE KENNEDY/CORBIS DOCUMENTARY VIA GETTY IMAGES

Part One

ROMANTIC BEACONS OF THE GATEWAY LAKE

Ontario

Lighthouses are among the most prominent and recognizable man-made structures on the planet. Precisely because of their status as navigational markers, they are closely identified with certain geographic or natural features. For instance, it is difficult to think of Ohio's Marblehead Peninsula as separate from the Marblehead Lighthouse or Ontario's Gibraltar Point as separate from the Gibraltar Point Lighthouse. Lighthouse towers seem almost the products of nature, as if they had been carved from native stone and left behind by the retreating glaciers of the last ice age. Of course, the Great Lakes themselves, which provide the reason for most of America's inland lighthouses, were in fact created by this chiseling action of ice and water on stone.

Each of the Earth's continents has at least one natural feature that stands out in our minds as a symbol for all its diverse lands and peoples. For Africa, that feature is probably the Nile River; for Asia, Mount Everest; for Australia, Ayers Rock; for South America, the Amazon Rainforest; for Europe, the Alps or perhaps the Greek Isles. But since most of us reading this book live in North America and have differing regional loyalties, the selection of such a symbol for this continent may seem a little more difficult. For instance, some might put forward the Mississippi River, while others may suggest Mount McKinley, the Colorado Rockies, or the California redwoods. Upon reflection, however, the available choices can easily be reduced to one.

A few miles from the City of Buffalo, New York, is a natural phenomenon so majestic and so powerful that every year it strikes millions of people speechless with awe. Tourists flock to see it from every state in the Union, every Canadian province, and, literally, every nation on Earth. Children the world over have heard of this place and, no doubt, dreamed of traveling to America to enjoy it for themselves. The phenomenon in question is, of course, Niagara Falls.

Actually a pair of falls, the American and Horseshoe, one on either side of the US–Canadian border, they form what is arguably the world's most popular and most visited natural wonder. And why not? Fed by the overflow from four of the Earth's largest lakes, the falls are very impressive indeed. More than 40 million gallons of water plunge over them every minute. This unforgettable display of nature's raw power has inspired poets, politicians, and countless ordinary people, not to mention generations of young couples who have flocked to the falls to celebrate, and consummate, their marriages.

Marriage of Waters

Why do the Niagara Falls exert such a pull on us? Maybe it is because they help us understand our place in the natural scheme of things. Certainly, the falls are a key to understanding the Great Lakes and the astounding geological forces that created them. Hundreds of millions of years ago, this region was covered by a warm, shallow sea teeming with life. Along the margins of the sea, colonies of tiny, shelled creatures piling one atop the other over millions of years built up an immense barrier reef. Eventually, the land was uplifted, the seas drained, and the ancient reef compacted into tough limestone.

Several times during the past million years, great sheets of ice, up to two miles thick, have pushed across the northern half of the continent. Like frozen bulldozers with blades one thousand miles wide, they scooped out basins. When the ice melted it filled the basins with water, forming lakes. But the stubborn limestone had resisted the ice and remained behind as a natural dike at the eastern end of Lake Erie. Today the waters of Erie, Huron, Michigan, and Superior spill over the dike, dropping several hundred feet in just a few miles on the way to Lake Ontario. The most dramatic descent is, of course, at Niagara, where the blue lake water plunges 184 feet over American Falls and 176 feet over Horseshoe Falls.

The Beaver Connection

Among the very first Europeans to see the falls was Samuel de Champlain, father of New France and founder of the City of Quebec. Champlain pushed up the St. Lawrence River, explored Lake Ontario, and may have reached Niagara as early as 1604, several years before the English established their first colony in Virginia at Jamestown.

No doubt the majesty of the falls impressed Champlain, but the French adventurer had much more to awe him besides: an entire pristine and unexplored New World. The Huron Native Americans told Champlain that beyond the falls lay several lakes even bigger than Ontario and a vast, wild region rich in furs and minerals. Initially, Champlain may have doubted their stories, but he and other astonished French explorers would soon learn that they were true. The falls were fed by an enormous system of swift-running rivers and huge lakes, reaching back 1,000 miles or more into the very heartland of the North American continent. The French quickly saw the potential of all these interconnected waterways—they could be used as a convenient and highly profitable commercial highway.

It has been said that, more than any human adventurer, the humble beaver deserves credit for opening up the North American interior. Much prized by hatmakers and the fashion-conscious ladies and gentlemen of Europe, beaver pelts gave tough French trappers a cash incentive for exploring America. Following every river and stream all the way to its source, they loaded sturdy bark canoes with pelts and then paddled and portaged them eastward along at least part of what is known today as the St. Lawrence Seaway.

It may be that the French built signal fires or placed lanterns on poles to guide their canoe freighters to key portages, villages, and fur-trading centers. It was the British, however, who would build the first true lighthouse on the Great Lakes. For more than 150 years, the British wrestled with the French for control of the lakes and the access they provided to the interior of the continent. This struggle reached its climax in 1759, during the French and Indian War, when an army of redcoats, under the command of General James Wolfe, appeared outside the city walls of Quebec. The marquis de Montcalm rushed out from behind the walls at the head of a poorly trained force of irregulars to confront Wolfe and was promptly defeated. Although both commanders were killed, the battle ended in near total defeat for the French. Having captured Quebec, the city of Champlain, the British took possession of Canada and the strategic Great Lakes waterways. But complete British dominion over the lakes would be short lived.

Revolutionary Ghost Ship

Only fifteen years after their victory over the French, the British found themselves once more at war in America. This time the fight was against their own unruly colonists. During this Revolutionary War the British maintained a powerful navy on the Great Lakes. Among their most formidable lake warships was HMS *Ontario*. Launched during the late spring of 1780, she was at least 80 feet long and square rigged like an oceangoing fighting ship. Armed with 16 six-pound cannon and six four-pounders, she had more than enough firepower to crush any American vessel that might challenge her mastery of Lake Ontario. The weather and the lake itself, however, could not be fought with cannon shot and gunpowder. The *Ontario* was destined to lose her only battle—with one of the Great Lakes' notorious autumn storms.

Late in October 1780 the *Ontario* weighed anchor and set sail from Niagara, bound for Oswego, New York, with a load of British soldiers, military supplies, and an army payroll chest brimming with gold and silver coins. On Halloween a gale came whistling out of the west, and by the time it had blown itself out the following morning, the *Ontario* was gone. Vanishing along with her were four women, five children, several Native American guides, and more than 70 soldiers and seamen. As with the *Edmund Fitzgerald* and so many other disappearances on the Great Lakes, this one remains a mystery to this day. Poignantly, settlers found dozens of British army caps bobbing in the waves along the south shore of the lake, but there were no other clues to the fate of the ship or its passengers, crew, and cargo. Treasure hunters, interested in valuable relics—not to mention the payroll chest—have searched endlessly for the wreck. Most believe the *Ontario* met her end near Thirty Mile Point. The discovery in 1954 of a very old anchor not far from the point lends weight to this opinion, but the ship herself has never been found.

Ironically, countless sailors may owe their lives indirectly to the sinking of the *Ontario*. The loss of this fine ship alerted British authorities to the need for better navigation markers on the Great Lakes. In 1781, the year after the Ontario disaster, they placed a light, fueled by whale oil, on the roof of Fort Niagara, at the mouth of the Niagara River. The French had built the old stone fortress in 1726 to help protect fur traders portaging their pelts from the upper lakes. The British had taken control of the fort after the French and Indian War. The fort and its light, the first established on the Great Lakes, became the property of the United States following the Revolutionary War.

The extraordinary tower was also one of the lake's most distinctive daymarks. Built during the mid-1890s, at the height of the Victorian era, it featured a decorative gallery and peaked roof suggestive of the elaborate helmet of a European cavalry officer.

Unfortunately, the old lighthouse weathered one too many of Lake Ontario's prodigious storms. By 1954 the structure had suffered damage so extensive the building itself became a safety hazard. The Coast Guard had no choice but to extinguish the light and pull down the top two-thirds of the tower, to keep it from falling under its own weight. Today the Braddock Point Lighthouse, with its squat, truncated tower, is a private residence closed to the public.

The privately owned, squared-off limestone tower of the Ogdensburg Lighthouse (opposite page) stands on the banks of the St. Lawrence River.
BENKRUT/ISTOCK VIA GETTY IMAGES

Ogdensburg Harbor Light
Ogdensburg, New York
1834

Located on the St. Lawrence River a few dozen miles from Lake Ontario, the town of Ogdensburg has been recognized by many as the gateway to the Great Lakes. Because of the strategic importance of this place, the French built a fort here in 1749. Founded by the famous French missionary Abbé François Picquet, Fort La Presentation served as a mission, trading center, and school as well as a key military outpost. The fort was burned and abandoned by its French defenders as British troops closed in during the final months of the French and Indian War.

On the ruins of La Presentation, the British built Fort Oswegatchie, which helped them control access to the Great Lakes during the Revolutionary War. Following the war, American troops under Colonel Samuel Ogden took possession of the fort. The thriving settlement that grew up here was later named for Ogden, and eventually, Ogdensburg became a vital St. Lawrence River port.

In 1834 a lighthouse was built on the site of the original French fort. The Ogdensburg Harbor Lighthouse was given a 65-foot limestone tower and spacious attached dwelling. Refurbished in 1900, the lighthouse still stands today. The light was inactive for many years but was restored to service in 2011 as a private aid to navigation.

How to Get There

Now on private property, the old light is off-limits to the public and can only be viewed from the water.

One of several prominent St. Lawrence River beacons, the Tibbett's Point Lighthouse (opposite page) near Cape Vincent, New York, marks the river entrance.

Tibbetts Point Light
Cape Vincent, New York
1827

Lighthouses are nearly always strategically located, but that is especially true of Tibbetts Point Lighthouse in Cape Vincent, New York. Its light marks the entrance to the St. Lawrence River and the beginning of the last leg of any journey from the Great Lakes to the Atlantic. Recognizing the importance of the place to commercial shipping, the US government placed a light station here in 1827. The stone tower stood 59 feet high and employed a whale-oil lamp and reflector lighting system.

The light tower seen at Cape Vincent today replaced the earlier lighthouse in 1854. Its 69-foot stucco tower was given a fourth-order Fresnel lens lit by a 50-candlepower oil lamp. A steam-powered fog signal began operation in 1896. The station was automated in 1981, but the beacon is still focused by its classic Fresnel lens.

How to Get There

Tibbett's Point and its lighthouse can be reached from Cape Vincent via Lighthouse Road. The grounds are open daily for walking, picnicking, and photography. For more information visit tibbettspointlighthouse.org or call (315) 654–2700.

Selkirk (Port Ontario) Light
Selkirk (Pulaski), New York
1838

Although its beacon served lake sailors for little more than 20 years, the Selkirk Lighthouse is one of the more fascinating and historic buildings on the Great Lakes. Built in 1838, it was taken out of service in 1859, when the local fishing and shipbuilding industries began to fade. Fortunately, the old lighthouse has survived. Its gabled fieldstone dwelling and old-style lantern are of considerable architectural and historical interest.

Built for $3,000 by local contractors from stone quarried nearby, the old dwelling is one of a kind. The small lantern room projecting through the roof is also highly unusual. It is of an early type in use before Fresnel lenses became common about the middle of the nineteenth century. Originally, the lantern held a 14-inch parabolic reflector and eight mineral-oil lamps. The light could be seen from about 14 miles out on the lake. Shortly before the lighthouse was discontinued, the outdated reflector system was replaced by a sixth-order Fresnel lens.

When the Salmon River began to silt up and ship traffic dropped off, the government saw little need for a light here. The building was eventually sold for use as a private residence and then as a hotel. Although its lantern was dark for more than 130 years, the old lighthouse is now back in operation. In 1989 the owners received permission from the Coast Guard to place an automated light in the lantern.

How to Get There

The lighthouse is located near the mouth of the Salmon River at the end of Lake Road to the west of Pulaski and Port Ontario This unique structure has been handsomely restored and is available for overnight accommodation. For more information visit salmonriverlighthousemarina.com.

Sodus Point Lighthouse
Sodus Point, New York
1825

On June 19, 1813, the citizens of sleepy Sodus Point, New York, had an uncharacteristically noisy day. A British fleet had sailed across Lake Ontario and rudely awakened them with cannon fire. The British fleet landed troops, but the redcoats were stopped and eventually driven off by a hastily gathered force of militia. To raise the alarm, a local horseman rode, Paul Revere style, through the countryside to warn farms and villages that "the British are coming."

From 1825 until just after the turn of the century, the Sodus Bay Lighthouse offered mariners a different sort of warning: Its bright beacon announced clearly that land was near. Completed during the administration of President John Quincy Adams, the rough split-stone tower and dwelling structures remained in use for more than 40 years. Following the Civil War they fell into a sad state of disrepair, and the government replaced them with the 45-foot-tall square stone tower and attached two-story dwelling that still stand here today. The light has been inactive since 1901, its job taken over by the nearby pier light.

How to Get There
The Sodus Point Lighthouse is off Ontario Street in the village of Sodus Point. Station structures house an excellent historical museum. For more information visit sodusbay lighthouse.org or call (315) 483–4936. Visitors will want to see the 3.5-order Fresnel lens in the tower.

Charlotte-Genesee Light
Rochester, New York
1822

Completed in 1822 at a cost of $3,301 and dropped from active service in 1881, the Charlotte-Genesee Lighthouse owes its continued existence in part to students of nearby Charlotte High School, who have made it their symbol. In 1965, when it was rumored the old lighthouse would be torn down, students at the school began a successful campaign to save the structure. Responding to student petitions, the government handed the lighthouse over to the Charlotte-Genesee Lighthouse Historical Society, which still maintains the venerable structure as a museum.

There is much history here to celebrate. Two centuries have passed since the 40-foot-high, octagonal limestone tower was erected on the edge of a bluff overlooking the mouth of the Genesee River and Lake Ontario beyond. David Denman, the station's first keeper, lived beside the tower in a rustic, two-room limestone cottage. Each night Denman trudged up the tower steps to light the ten Argand lamps that produced the light concentrated by a set of reflectors. These relatively inefficient reflectors were exchanged for a fourth-order Fresnel lens in 1852. The current two-and-a-half-story brick dwelling replaced the cottage in 1863. In 1974 the Genesee Lighthouse was placed on the National Register of Historic Places.

How to Get There
Lake Avenue in Rochester leads to Charlotte, Holy Cross Church, and the lighthouse. While the grounds are open daily, the lighthouse and dwelling are open to the public on weekends. For more information visit geneseelighthouse.org or call (585) 621–6179.

Thirty Mile Point Light
Somerset, New York
1875

Located on the south shore of Lake Ontario about 30 miles from the mouth of the Niagara River, the distinctive Thirty Mile Point Lighthouse has been featured on a US postage stamp.

Located on Golden Hill, on a point of land 30 miles east of the mouth of the Niagara River, the square stone tower of Thirty Mile Point Lighthouse rises 78 feet above the surface of Lake Ontario. The scenic point on which the lighthouse stands is memorable, not only because it is a convenient mile marker but also because of the waves of history that have continually washed over this place.

In 1678 a 20-ton sailing vessel under the command of the French explorer Sieur de La Salle wrecked here. A century later, during the Revolutionary War, the British fighting ship HMS *Ontario* was believed to have gone down near Thirty Mile Point, with the loss of 88 lives. A two-master armed with heavy cannon, the *Ontario* was carrying British troops to fight continental forces in New York, as well as an army payroll estimated at $15,000, when she foundered during a blizzard.

Some say that Golden Hill takes its name from the glittering army payroll supposedly washed or brought ashore from the wreck and buried. There have been no few unsuccessful attempts to dig up the treasure. A less dramatic explanation for the name, which has the support of local historians, is the profusion of goldenrod that once bloomed on an island off the point. Yet rumors of buried treasure at Golden Hill persist.

The Thirty Mile Point Lighthouse was built on Golden Hill in 1875, at a cost of $90,000. It remained in service until 1959, when the light was automated and transferred to a slender steel tower nearby. The gray square-cut stones of the original tower were shipped from Chaumont Bay near the St. Lawrence River and then hauled up the steep banks of Golden Hill.

A Fresnel lens manufactured in France was installed in the eight-foot-wide lantern room. The handmade French lens concentrated the light produced by a kerosene flame so effectively that the light could be seen from more than 18 miles away. In 1885 the kerosene flame was replaced with one of the earliest electric bulbs ever put in a lighthouse.

How to Get There

Thirty Mile Point Lighthouse is the main attraction of Golden Hill State Park, which is north of Lower Lake Road in the town of Somerset. The park offers campsites, picnic tables, a marina, and an engaging nature trail. Visitors can take a self-guided tour of the lighthouse. For more information visit parks.ny.gov or call (716) 795–3885.

Fort Niagara Light
Youngstown, New York
1781

Located in Youngstown, New York, where the Niagara River meets Lake Ontario, the Fort Niagara Lighthouse stands as a mute reminder of early struggles for economic and political dominance in North America. Now an automated light station, the stone building attached to the tower is leased from the Coast Guard by the Old Fort Niagara Association, which uses it as a museum and gift shop. Having served three nations (France, Britain, and the United States) Old Fort Niagara is now a New York State Park that memorializes the grit and persistence of those who explored, fought for, and settled the New World. These achicvements are celebrated at Fort Niagara State Park living-history exhibits and numerous military reenactments held here during the summer.

How to Get There
From Niagara, New York, the Robert Moses Parkway leads to the park entrance. Inside the park, signs point the way to the lighthouse. For more information visit oldfortniagara.org or call (716) 745–7611.

Part Two

ROMANTIC BEACONS OF THE WARRIOR LAKE

Erie

Lighthouses serve the mariners of all nations but because they are built and maintained by governments, they are closely linked to political history. They have played important roles in the prosecution of war and in the making of nations. This is especially true of the United States, which has been a world leader as a builder of lighthouses. The United States has more lighthouses along its inland shores (the shores of the Great Lakes) than most nations have on their entire ocean coastlines. This might not have been true, though, except for a rare freshwater naval battle fought more than two centuries ago.

Buckskins and Tomahawks

On a September afternoon in 1813, backwoodsmen and farmers living in the remote northwestern corner of Ohio might have thought a storm had broken far out over the waters of Lake Erie. So it had, but the booming they heard in the distance was no natural thunder. Rather, it was the roar of cannon, and the "storm" was a mighty sea battle being fought nearly 500 miles from the nearest salt water. Somewhere out there on the lake, a flotilla of heavily armed American warships and an equally powerful British fleet were slugging it out with steel and lead for control of Lake Erie and of the entire Great Lakes region.

One of only a very few naval engagements ever fought in fresh water, this extraordinary confrontation also proved to have been one of history's most decisive battles. The chain of events leading up to the battle of Lake Erie began in a most unlikely way: with a bloody musket-and-tomahawk clash between buckskinned frontiersmen and Native Americans in war paint. In 1811 an army of pioneers, commanded by a flamboyant general named William Henry Harrison, ran head-on into a large Native American war party led by the legendary Tecumseh and his brother, "The Prophet." The battle erupted along an otherwise placid Indiana creek known to the Native Americans as Tippecanoe. When it was over Tecumseh and his braves had been driven off, leaving behind many dead and a considerable number of British muskets.

Harrison's victory left an indelible mark on history. It opened the Midwestern states of Ohio, Indiana, and Illinois to a flood of white settlers, who now felt relatively safe from the Native Americans. It launched Harrison on a successful military and political career, which 30 years afterward would land him in the White House as the ninth president of the United States. In fact, Harrison campaigned for the presidency on the slogan "Tippecanoe and Tyler Too," a phrase that, to this day, still twists the tongues of grammar-school history students. But the battle's most immediate effect was to inflame American public opinion against the British, who were accused of supplying weapons to hostile western tribes. The anti-British sentiment grew to such a fever pitch that war was declared the following summer.

The decision to make war on the world's dominant naval power would quickly prove a disastrous one. The British swept American shipping from the seas, sealed off eastern ports, and even burned the White House and the Capitol in Washington, D.C. But for a brash 28-year-old naval lieutenant and his ragtag fleet on Lake Erie, the British might also have snatched away the vast lands to the south and west of the Great Lakes and given them to Canada.

When Lieutenant Oliver Hazard Perry arrived in Ohio during the autumn of 1812, he had no ships to command. His assignment of driving an already established British fleet from Lake Erie seemed hopeless. Perry's warships had to be built from scratch, using raw timber felled right on the shores of the lake.

As his small party of shipwrights and seamen labored around the clock, Perry kept a wary eye on the lakeward horizon. He was watching for sails signaling the British attack that he was sure was coming to burn his unfinished ships, destroy his makeshift shipyard, and scatter his tiny force into the wilderness. But as construction of the American fleet continued, month after weary month, the British held back.

Commanding the British naval forces on the lake was Captain Robert Barclay, a veteran of the famed battle of Trafalgar. Barclay felt secure at his base in Detroit, Michigan, and perhaps he took his young opponent too lightly. For whatever reason, Barclay never attacked, and by the summer of 1813, Perry was able to complete and launch eight ships.

Presque Isle Lighthouse
near Erie, Pennsylvania.

Early in September the American commander made his move. Having sailed his small fleet to the west end of Lake Erie, Perry blockaded the mouth of the Detroit River and cut off British supplies. Soon Barclay was forced to sail out and meet Perry on the open waters of the lake.

We Have Met the Enemy

The battle, fought just to the west of Put-in-Bay and north of what is today the city of Sandusky, Ohio, commenced shortly before noon on September 10. The British cannon had longer range and began to blast away before the American ships could reply. But a favorable shift in the wind brought the two lines of embattled ships close together and allowed Perry's heavier short-range cannon to pound his foes. Perry had filled the rigging of his largest vessels, the *Lawrence* and *Niagara*, with Kentucky long-riflemen, and their hawkeyed sharpshooting picked off key British officers one by one. Although he would survive the battle, even Barclay fell, seriously wounded, on the deck of his flagship, the *Detroit*. By midafternoon the British were forced to strike their colors, and Perry, who would forever afterwards be known as "Commodore Perry," was able to send his famous message back to the American shores: *We have met the enemy and they are ours; two ships, two brigs, one schooner, and one sloop.*

Destruction of Barclay's fleet made it possible for General Harrison to march on Detroit and clear American territory of British outposts. In October he defeated the retreating British and their Native American allies, in a bitterly contested battle on Canadian soil. The entire British force was either killed or captured, and the charismatic Tecumseh was cut down while making a courageous last stand with his braves.

Harrison's success on land, combined with Perry's victory out on Lake Erie, likely saved the Great Lakes states for the Americans. Without those states and the access to their vital inland waterways, the United States certainly would have been a much different, and poorer, country. By 1841, when Harrison became president, commerce generated by the Great Lakes region was already producing an economic boom. The Erie Canal linked the lakes to the Hudson and the Atlantic seaboard while a growing string of lighthouses led freighters and passenger steamers from Buffalo to Detroit and beyond.

As president, Harrison might have pushed for even more economic growth in the Great Lakes region—perhaps ordering the construction of additional lighthouses—but he never got the chance. It rained on the day he took the oath of office. 67 years old and in fragile health, Harrison was no longer the robust frontier soldier he had been during the War of 1812. While making what turned out to be the longest inauguration speech in history, he caught a severe cold. Ironically, little more than a month after taking office, the hero of Tippecanoe died from a fatal case of the sniffles.

Dunkirk Light
Point Gratiot, New York
1827

Dunkirk Lighthouse rises from a 20-foot-high bluff at Point Gratiot, southwest of the Erie Canal terminus in Buffalo. Today it still throws its guiding beam across Lake Erie, just as it once did for nineteenth-century immigrant ships bound for the upper Great Lakes. Although its light helped keep vessels on course, it could not always prevent tragedy.

The first light at Dunkirk Harbor was commissioned in 1826, only a few years after one of the earliest recorded disasters on Lake Erie. Launched in 1818 at Black Rock, New York, the paddle wheeler *Walk-in-the-Water* was the lake's first steamboat. But the power of steam could not overcome the forces of nature, and in October 1818, this famous steamboat foundered on a sandbar in heavy weather. Fortunately, no lives were lost, but only the vessel's big steam engines could be salvaged from the wreck.

As the sun drops down beneath the Lake Erie horizon, New York's historic Point Gratiot (Dunkirk) beacon comes to life just as it has for nearly two centuries.

The first lighthouse at Gratiot Point, which became popularly known as Lighthouse Point, was completed in 1827 by Buffalo contractor Jesse Peck. It stood a short distance from the current 61-foot-high tower, which replaced it in 1875.

Early attempts were made here to substitute natural gas for the whale oil typically used to fuel lighthouse lamps. These experiments were not successful, however. In 1857 the lantern was fitted with a third-order Fresnel lens, which produced a 15,000-candlepower flash every 90 seconds. The light could be seen from 17 miles offshore.

Today the light station at Point Gratiot serves as a military memorial as well as a lighthouse museum. Point Gratiot is believed to be named for Charles Gratiot, the same U.S. Army engineer for whom Fort Gratiot, on Michigan's St. Clair River, is named.

How to Get There

Located in Dunkirk off Route 5, which parallels the lakeshore just northwest of the New York State Thruway (I–90), the Dunkirk Lighthouse is open daily throughout the year. The seven-room keeper's house now serves as one of the best lighthouse museums on the Great Lakes. For more information visit dunkirklighthouse.com or call (716) 366–5050.

Presque Isle Light
Erie, Pennsylvania
1819

Originally, Pennsylvania had no shore frontage on Lake Erie, but the farsighted people of that friendly state recognized the importance of access to America's strategic inland seas. So immediately after the Revolutionary War, they bought a 45-mile stretch of beaches and inlets, including what turned out to be a very attractive and historic harbor. It was at Erie, Pennsylvania, that Perry and his shipwrights built the modest flotilla of warships that defeated the powerful Great Lakes fleet of the British during the War of 1812.

Perhaps it was partly in memory of that victory, as well as in recognition of the growing importance of Erie as a port, that the government built on of the earliest Great Lakes lighthouses on the Presque Isle Peninsula in 1819. In French, the term *presque isle* means "almost or nearly an island." The lighthouse seen here today was built in 1873 and fitted with a fourth-order Fresnel lens displaying a fixed white light. The 68-foot-tall square tower placed the focal plane of the light 73 feet above the lake's surface. The original Fresnel lens has been replaced by an automated beacon.

How to Get There
The Presque Isle Lighthouse is in Presque Isle State Park at the end of a seven-mile finger of sand stretching into Lake Erie. From Route 5 in Erie. Visitors follow Peninsula Drive 11 miles north to the park entrance. For more information visit presqueisle lighthouse.org or call (814) 833–3604.

Fairport Harbor Light
Fairport, Ohio
1825

The light station at Fairport was completed in the fall of 1825, the same year that the Erie Canal opened, connecting the Great Lakes with the Hudson River and the port of New York. Fairport's first lighthouse was built on the east side of the Grand River by Jonathan Goldsmith, a Connecticut native who had moved to Ohio in 1811. The original brick tower was 30 feet high, with supporting walls three feet thick at the ground and 20 inches thick at the top. The tower was given an eleven-foot-diameter soapstone deck and capped with an octagonal iron lantern. The two-story keeper's house had spacious rooms, each with plastered walls, three windows, and a fireplace. There were also a sizable kitchen and cellar. The first keeper to live and work here was Samuel Butler.

By midcentury both the tower and keeper's cottage had badly deteriorated, and in 1869 Congress appropriated $30,000 to replace them. By August 1871 the station's third-order Fresnel lens had been installed in a new sandstone tower, where it shined for more than half a century.

On June 9, 1925, a new combination light and foghorn station was put in operation, and the federal government announced that it would raze the old lighthouse. Local appeals to save the historic structure succeeded, and in 1941 the village of Fairport leased the lighthouse from the Coast Guard. Today the Fairport Harbor Historical Society maintains the lighthouse as a marine museum.

How to Get There
The lighthouse and museum are on the northwest corner of Second and High Streets in the village of Fairport Harbor. The museum in the old keeper's dwelling includes a wonderful collection of artifacts from the early days of the Lighthouse Service and a variety of other maritime exhibits. For more information visit fairportharborlighthouse.org or call (440) 354–4825.

Lorain West Breakwater Light
Lorain, Ohio
1917

Seldom is a town so closely identified with its lighthouse as Lorain, Ohio. "It's our symbol," said one longtime resident. "New York City has the Statue of Liberty, and we have our lighthouse."

That has been the case for a long time. For at least 150 years, beacons have guided vessels to Lorain. During the early 1800s this important job was done by a simple lantern hung from a pole. But by 1837 the town had its own official lighthouse: a wooden tower rising from the end of a harbor pier. The beautiful lighthouse seen here today dates to 1917 when it was built by the U.S. Army Corps of Engineers. It served Lorain and ships moving along the south shore of Lake Erie until 1965 when a fully automated breakwater light was established on a nearby pier.

Fortunately, the beautiful 1917 lighthouse has been preserved as a monument to the town and the generations of keepers who maintained the light. Although nowadays the Lorain Lighthouse serves mariners only as a daymark, it remains an an inspiration to the people of the town.

How to Get There

From US Highway 6, Oberlin Avenue provides access to the parking area at Lorain's municipal pier. A good view of the lighthouse can be had from the north end of the parking area and from several other points along the Lake Erie shore.

Marblehead Light
Bay Point, Ohio
1821

Built in 1821, Marblehead Lighthouse is the oldest active navigational light on the Great Lakes. The Marblehead beacon has flashed out over a lot of history since it was placed in service, only a few years after Perry won his decisive victory over the British at the Battle of Lake Erie. This key naval battle was fought just north of the north of Marblehead in September 1813, but that was not the last time war would touch the area.

During the Civil War, thousands of captured Confederate soldiers languished in a 300-acre prison on Johnson's Island, within sight of Marblehead. They could see the flashing Marblehead Light every night, and perhaps they sometimes felt it was calling them home to South. Eventually, they would go home, and along with their memories of prison and of a distant beacon calling out to them at night, they carried home the rules of a new sport: baseball. At Johnson Island, the prisoners had formed a team and they often defeated the Yankee teams who came to Johnson Island to play them.

Of course, the Marblehead beacon has always been of far more consequence to mariners on Lake Erie than to imprisoned soldiers, and over its more than two centuries of service it has guided countless vessels large and small and saved hundreds, if not thousands, of lives. During all that time, the old stone tower has changed very little. Late in the nineteenth century, its height was raised from 55 to 65 feet, but otherwise it looks much as it has since 1821. Fitted with a fourth-order Fresnel lens, it displays a flashing green light.

How to Get There

The Marblehead Lighthouse is so historic and impressive that it merits its own state park. The lighthouse and six-acre park are located just off East Main Street in Marblehead a few miles east of Port Clinton, Ohio. For more information visit marblehead lighthouseohio.org.

Toledo Harbor Light
Toledo, Ohio
1904

Mariners seeing the Toledo Harbor Lighthouse for the first time or watching as it emerges mysteriously from one of Lake Erie's thick fogbanks must rub their eyes and look again. Chocolate-colored brick walls, Romanesque arches, and a bulging round-edged roof make this lighthouse an architectural wonder. It is hard to say exactly what storybook fantasy the structure was intended to suggest—perhaps part Victorian palace and part Russian Orthodox church. But for all its fancifulness, the old lighthouse is a hardworking lake veteran: It has served faithfully since 1904.

Shortly before the turn of the twentieth century, the Army Corps of Engineers dredged a channel from Lake Erie into the Maumee River. This opened Toledo to an influx of deepwater freighter traffic. To mark the channel and point the way to the city's busy harbor, the corps built a lighthouse about eight miles out in the lake from Toledo. The design was, no doubt, some military engineer's concept of a stylish building.

With their usual zeal for solid construction, the corpsmen established the structure on a massive concrete-and-stone crib rising almost 20 feet above the water. They gave it stout brick walls three stories high and pushed the light tower up through the center of the roof. They filled the lantern room atop the tower with a state-of-the-art, rotating Fresnel lens. With a focal plane more than 70 feet above the lake, the Fresnel's alternating red-and-white flashes could be seen from sixteen miles away. Although automated since 1965, the station remains active.

Like many other old lighthouses around the country, this one is said to be haunted. Considering the look of the place, it would be surprising if the building were not haunted. Some say, however, that the stories of a phantom can be traced to U.S. Coast Guard efforts to discourage vandalism at the station. Following removal of the last keeper in 1965, the Coast Guard placed a fully uniformed mannequin in one of the lower windows to serve as a scarecrow.

How to Get There

The only satisfactory way to see the lighthouse is from a boat, as the station is off-limits to visitors. The light's distinctive red-and-white flash, however, can be seen from many points along the Toledo shoreline. For more information visit toledoharborlight house.org.

Part Three

ROMANTIC BEACONS OF THE THUNDER LAKE

Huron

Why build lighthouses along the shores of the Great Lakes? For guidance. These lakes are no ordinary bodies of fresh water. They are enormous inland seas hundreds of miles in length. Sailors here need lighthouses to guide them, especially where low headlands offer few distinctive features. "It's like trying to navigate in a wheat field," said one frustrated sea captain after he brought his oceangoing freighter down the length of the St. Lawrence Seaway. But the Great Lakes lighthouses serve an even more important function: They save lives. On the wind-torn waters of these lakes, safety is a vitally important consideration, and sailors keep a close eye on the weather. In a storm, lighthouses provide mariners with a comforting visual anchor.

The Storms of November

November brings a marrow-deep chill to the bones of sailors on the Great Lakes. It's not just that the weather gets colder (it does, usually) but also that the lakes themselves take on a different character. They turn tempestuous and develop sharp, unpredictable tempers. Storms can blacken their faces in a matter of minutes and churn their waters into a confusion of towering waves capable of breaking a ship in half.

As the lakes change mood, so do the titanic commercial shipping enterprises they support. Captains and crews work overtime, hurrying to make one last trip; draw one last paycheck; or deliver one last cargo of iron, steel, oil, corn, or wheat before the witch of winter locks the lakes in a crush of unbreakable ice.

Tired sailors pushing themselves and their ships to the limit make a habit of looking back over their shoulders. They are watching for November—not the one on the calendar but the one that comes calling when you least expect it. Among Great Lakes sailors it is sometimes said that "Thanksgiving comes only if you survive November." They have endless tales of tragedy to prove the point: the November that took the *Edmund Fitzgerald* in 1975, the November that took the *Bradley* in 1958, and scores of other Novembers that sent stout ships and strong crews to the bottom. But when old lake sailors gather to tell stories of the calamities brought on by the year's eleventh month, there is one November they rarely leave out: November 1913.

Those who were superstitious about numbers said it would be an unlucky year; but up until the fall, 1913 had proved them wrong. The spring and summer had been kind to the Great Lakes, providing bathers, lovers, and sailors with a seemingly endless string of warm, clear days and calm, starry nights. Business was booming, and the large and growing fleet of freighters operating on the lakes set records for shipping.

Then came October and, with it, high winds howling out of the west. A record cold snap sent temperatures plunging below zero, and a series of early snowstorms dusted the lakes' shores with white. But for all its chill and bluster, October's unexpected outburst did little damage—a broken rudder here, a severed anchor chain there, and a couple of old wooden steamers run aground.

The year's fourth and final quarter had gotten off to an ominous start; but with lucrative contracts in their hands, captains were not willing to tie up their vessels for the season. They pushed themselves, their ships, and their crews harder than ever. They were determined to finish the work that they had begun in the spring and continued so successfully during the summer, attempting to make 1913 the best year ever for shipping on the Great Lakes. But it was not to be.

At first November seemed likely to reverse the unsettling trend of the previous month. For a week, gentle breezes rippled the lakes, and the temperatures were downright balmy. But experienced sailors knew these pleasant conditions would not hold for long, not at this time of year, and how right they were. Even as they hung up their uniform jackets to enjoy the unseasonable temperatures in shirtsleeves while their freighters cut through glass-smooth water, three deadly weather systems were headed their way. One rushed in with freezing winds from the Bering Sea; another poured over the Rockies, carrying an immense load of water from as far off as the South Pacific; and a third came spinning up, cyclone style, from the Caribbean. The three slammed into one another over the Great Lakes on or about November 7, 1913, creating what was in effect an inland hurricane.

This extraordinary storm struck with little or no warning. Dozens of freighters were caught in in the middle of the lake, far from safe anchorage or, worse, near ship-killing rocks, shoals, and shallows. High waves battered hulls, and freezing spray caked decks and wheelhouses in a thick layer of ice. Swirling snow squalls blinded captains, pilots, and navigators, while high winds drove their vessels ever closer to disaster. The storm raged on without pause for five long days. By the time that the clouds broke and the winds died down, on November 12, more than 40 ships had been wrecked, their hulls shattered by the waves or ripped open on shoals. Down with them went 235 sailors and passengers. Only a few of the bodies were ever recovered.

Good-by Nellie

On Lake Erie the 187-ton *Lightship No. 82* was blown off her mooring and bowled over by the waves. All six crewmen were lost. Before he drowned, Captain Hugh Williams apparently scratched a hurried farewell to his wife on a piece of wood and set it adrift. A waterlogged board later found washed up on a beach in New York held this message: "Good-by Nellie, ship breaking up fast. Williams."

Up on Lake Superior the tramp freighter *Leafield* was driven onto rocks and torn to pieces. All eighteen members of the crew were lost. Also lost on Superior was the 525-foot ore freighter *Henry B. Smith*. In a tragic lapse of judgment and prudent seamanship, Captain Jimmy Owen took the *Smith* out of the relative safety of Marquette Harbor and steamed directly into the teeth of the storm. Only a few scattered pieces of wreckage, and none of the ship's 23 crewmen, were ever found.

It was on Lake Huron, however, that the storm vented its full fury. When the storm first assaulted Huron on November 7, its shipping lanes were filled with vessels crossing northwestward toward Michigan and Superior or southeastward toward Erie. As darkness set in, lighthouse beacons called to these ships from many points along the Michigan shore. There were safe harbors in this storm, and the lights marked the way. But most ships could not reach them or make any headway at all against the fierce westerly winds. Many captains pointed their bows toward the northeast and made a run for the Canadian side, where they hoped to find some protection. Many never made it.

Huron's mountainous waves chewed up dozens of ships, and the lake's deep waters swallowed them whole. At least eight large freighters—the *McGean*, *Carruthers*, *Hydrus*, *Wexford*, *Scott*, *Regina*, *Price*, and *Argus*—all disappeared from the lake without a trace. Vanishing with them were 178 passengers and crewmen.

Fort Gratiot Light
Port Huron, Michigan
1825

Established in 1825, the Fort Gratiot Light Station is Michigan's oldest—older, in fact, than the state itself, which was admitted to the Union in 1837. The station still watches over the Lake Huron entrance to the St. Clair River.

The first keeper of the Fort Gratiot Lighthouse was George McDougal, a Detroit lawyer who won his appointment through political influence. His was not that desirable a job, however, as McDougal depleted his personal savings keeping the station habitable. The tower was not built to government specifications, and the materials used were shoddy. McDougal considered it unsafe, and he was quite right. The shaky tower soon collapsed, and a more robust structure replaced it in 1829. Today, two centuries after McDougal served here, the 82-foot tower still guides mariners, but its light has been automated since 1933.

How to Get There
Located on Omar Street at the east end of Garfield Street in Port Huron, the Fort Gratiot Lighthouse serves as both an active light station and the focus of a popular maritime museum. For more information on the Fort Gratiot Lighthouse or the nearby Lightship Huron, visit phmuseum.org or call (810) 982–0891.

Port Sanilac Light
Port Sanilac, Michigan
1886

Established in 1886, the Port Sanilac beacon was a key link in the 300-mile-long chain of navigational lights that once guided vessels along Michigan's Lake Huron shore. It was among the first lights mariners saw as they exited the St. Clair River and steamed northward into the lake.

As with lighthouses everywhere, the Port Sanilac station has lost much of its importance as a navigational aid. However, the light remains in operation and can still be seen each night. Beaming out over the lake from atop its 69-foot octagonal tower, the beacon is visible from a distance of 16 miles.

Although located on private property and closed to the public, the Port Sanilac Light remains a fully operational navigational beacon.

HAVESEEN/ISTOCK VIA GETTY IMAGES

The station's unusual step-sided, brick keeper's dwelling is now a private residence. The brick tower is painted white and flares outward near the top, giving it the appearance of an enormous chess piece.

How to Get There

Now a private residence, the lighthouse is off-limits to the public. However, the striking tower and dwelling can be viewed and photographed from a nearby breakwater that can be accessed from Cherry in Port Sanilac. For more information visit portsanilaclighthouse.com.

Point aux Barques Lighthouse was intended to warn vessels away from a deadly shoal just offshore. JOSHUA BOZARTH VIA GETTY IMAGES

Pointe aux Barques Light
Port Austin, Michigan
1848

The French called the place Pointe aux Barques, or "point of little boats," perhaps because of the many canoes brought here by fur traders. This strategic headland marks a key turning point from Lake Huron into Saginaw Bay. Recognizing its importance to shipping, the government chose Pointe aux Barques as the site for one of the tallest and most powerful lighthouses on the Great Lakes.

Completed in 1848 at a cost of $5,000, the original stone structure proved inadequate and had to be rebuilt less than ten years later. In 1857 it was replaced with an impressive 89-foot brick tower and fitted with a state-of-the-art, third-order Fresnel lens. Today this beautiful old lens can be seen at the Grice Museum in Port Austin. Its work is now being done by a million-candlepower automated beacon. The flashing white light can be seen from about 18 miles out on Lake Huron.

How to Get There

The Pointe aux Barques Lighthouse is in a county park off Lighthouse Road, about 10 miles east of Port Austin and six miles north of Port Hope. The tower is generally not open to the public, but park visitors enjoy excellent views of the light. The park offers a campground and picnic area. For more information visit pointauxbarqueslighthouse .org or call (586) 243–1838.

HAVESEEN/ISTOCK VIA GETTY IMAGES

Tawas Point Light
Tawas City, Michigan
1853

The thumb of Michigan's mitten is created by a long, southwestern extension of Lake Huron called Saginaw Bay. By the middle of the nineteenth century, the bay had become commercially strategic, and lighthouse officials saw the need to mark its entrance. In 1848 they placed a lighthouse at Pointe aux Barques on the south side of the entrance, and five years later another was built at Ottawa Point (now known as Tawas Point) on the north side.

The Tawas Point Lighthouse was completed and in operation by 1853, but its beacon served mariners for little more than 20 years. Lake Huron constantly reshapes certain sections of its shoreline, and, by the 1870s, sandy Tawas Point had grown so much that the lighthouse stood more than a mile from the waters of the lake. To correct this problem a 67-foot tower was built closer to the lake in 1876. The conical tower is painted white and topped by a black-iron lantern room. The flashing white beacon is produced by a rotating fourth-order Fresnel lens.

How to Get There
The lighthouse is in Tawas Point State Park a mile or so west of Tawas City. From the beachside parking area, a walking path leads to the lighthouse. For more information visit michigan.gov/mhc/museums/tawas or call (517) 930–3806. Camping facilities and picnic tables are available in the park.

Sturgeon Point Light
Alcona, Michigan
1870

Beaming from the top of a 68 foot light tower, Sturgeon Point Lighthouse has saved many lives since it was placed in service in 1870. Today the light continues to guide mariners and warn them away from a nearby ship-killing reef. Although the light station remains active, it serves primarily as a museum. Occasionally, visitors can climb the 85 steps of the tower's cast-iron stairway.

A close look at the structures on Sturgeon Point (above) and Tawas Point (opposite page) miles to the north suggests these two Michigan lighthouses were built using the same set of plans. Both feature a brick tower just under 70 feet in height and similar, attached brick cottages.

Standing beside the 3.5-order lens inside the lantern room and gazing out across the lake, one is reminded of the life-and-death dramas that have taken place in this dangerous stretch of water. Among those was the loss of the wooden steamer *Marine City* near Sturgeon Point in 1880. Fire ravaged the freighter, which sank along with a heavy load of shingles and 20 passengers including three stowaways.

There have been many wrecks along these shores. For instance, in October 1887 the 233-ton schooner *Venus* foundered off the nearby Black River with a loss of seven lives and load of massive grindstones. In 1924, the freighter *Clifton* was lost nearby during a fierce September gale.

How to Get There

From Highway 23 just north of Harrisville, Michigan, Lake Shore Drive and Point Road provide access to Sturgeon Point State Park and the lighthouse. For more information visit alconahistoricalsociety.com or call (989) 471–2088.

The Middle Island Lighthouse (opposite page) with its distinctive red band is owned and maintained by local lighthouse preservationists. Located about 10 miles north of Alpena, Michigan, the 78-foot tower still displays its third-order beacon every evening.

Middle Island Light
North of Alpena, Michigan
1905

Although abandoned by the U.S. Coast Guard years ago, this remarkable island light station has been given new life as a monument to our nation's maritime heritage. Many orphaned lighthouses quickly fall into ruin, but this one has been taken under the wing of an energetic local preservationist organization known as the Middle Island Lighthouse Keepers Association. Based in nearby Alpena, this hardworking group has restored the station to its original appearance.

The banded, conical brick tower is crowned with an iron gallery and lantern room. The powerful beacon shining from the top of the tower was intended to guide vessels along the northeastern shores of the lower peninsula. It pointed the way toward the Straits of Mackinac providing access to Lake Michigan and to the vital locks at Sault Ste. Marie, opening the way to Lake Superior.

How to Get There
Located on an island about two miles offshore, the historic tower, residence, and other buildings are accessible only by boat. However, summer excursions are available. For more information visit middleislandlighthouse.com.

Presque Isle Light
Presque Isle, Michigan
1840

The current, still active Presque Isle Light shines from atop one of the tallest navigational towers on the Great Lakes. The 113-foot light tower provides the beacon with sufficient height to reach ships as much as 25 miles away. In addition to its maritime duties, the soaring tower and attached rectangular brick keeper's house serves as the centerpiece for a 100-acre public park maintained by Presque Isle Township. The park also includes an earlier Presque Isle Lighthouse, which was completed in 1840 and discontinued in 1871, when the new tower was completed. There are also range lights, which were used to mark the harbor channel. These venerable structures occupy a cedar- and pine-covered peninsula that helps form Presque Isle Harbor on one side and North Bay on the other side.

Typically, the active lighthouse is referred to as the *New* Presque Isle Light while its predecessor is known as the *Old* Presque Isle Light, but of course, these terms are relative. Consider that in 1885 Thomas Garrity took over as keeper from his father Patrick Garrity, who had held the same job since the Civil War. The younger Garrity remained the official keeper until 1935, a remarkable 50-year tenure.

Perhaps not surprisingly, the Old Presque Isle Lighthouse is said to be haunted. A persistent story holds that a ghost, said to be that of a keeper's wife, walks the steps of the tower, particularly at night. As the story goes, she was driven insane by the isolation of her husband's remote duty station. It is said that on windy nights her lonely calls can still be heard.

How to Get There

Both lighthouses can be reached via Grand Lake Road in Presque Isle, Michigan. For more information visit michigan.org/property/new-presque-isle-lighthouse-park-and -museum or call (989) 787–0814.

Forty Mile Point Light
Rogers City, Michigan
1897

Nearly lost among the trees at the edge of a broad, sandy beach, the squarish Forty Mile Point tower guards a long and otherwise unmarked stretch of Michigan's Lake Huron shoreline.

Until the late 1890s the 50-mile stretch of shoreline between Cheboygan and Presque Isle Lighthouse was dark and threatening to mariners. Here was a dangerous gap in an otherwise almost unbroken chain of navigational lights guiding ships through the Great Lakes. Completed in 1896, Forty Mile Point Lighthouse was intended to fill that gap.

Still in use, the square brick tower stands 53 feet tall. At the top an octagonal, black-trimmed cast-iron lantern housing a fourth-order Fresnel lens that displays a flashing white light. Painted white, the tower stands in sharp contrast to the attached natural-brick keeper's dwelling which features a pair of gables, one on either side of the tower. The station also has a well-preserved brick oil house and fog-signal building.

How to Get There
The well-maintained tower, dwelling, and other structures are not open to the public, but the grounds and buildings are quite beautiful. For more information visit forty milepointlighthouse.org or call (989) 734–4907.

Part Four

ROMANTIC BEACONS OF THE ALL-AMERICAN LAKE

Michigan

Lake Michigan is about 30 percent smaller than Lake Superior and slightly smaller than Lake Huron, but with a surface area of 22,300 square miles, it nonetheless ranks fifth largest among all the freshwater lakes in the world. With a length of more than 400 miles, a width of 120 miles, and a maximum depth of nearly 1,000 feet, Lake Michigan stores about 1,200 cubic miles of water, enough to supply the City of Chicago at current use rates for about a million years. But what is most notable about this enormous lake is the fact that every one of its 1,400 miles of shoreline is located within the United States of America. If you are from the United States, you don't need a passport or a trip to Canada to see this lake—it's all American.

The King of Lake Michigan

Over the centuries since La Salle first sailed the Great Lakes in his hardy little sailing ship *Griffin*, many have traveled in his wake to Lake Michigan, seeking earthly and even heavenly rewards. One such adventurer was a Mormon outlaw named James Jesse Strang, who came to Michigan's Beaver Island during the mid-1800s and proclaimed himself king of the place. Like some religious radicals of our own time, Strang and his fervent band obeyed few earthly laws and had a penchant for violence.

Not surprisingly, Strang's non-Mormon neighbors felt threatened by his activities, which apparently included theft of supplies, weapons, and livestock. One of Strang's raiding parties even attacked the Grand Traverse Lighthouse on Cat Head, but his men were driven away by federal marshals before they could remove its Fresnel lens. Conflict was inevitable, and open warfare soon erupted, spreading throughout the Michigan islands and spilling over onto the mainland. The fighting came to end on June 16, 1857, when Strang was gunned down by Thomas Bedford, one of his own disgruntled followers.

On June 16, 1887, 30 years to the day after her father had assassinated the "King of the Lake," Minnie Bedford boarded the steamer *Champlain* in Norwood, Michigan, for the evening run to nearby Charlevoix. The entire Strang affair, although legendary, was now far in the past, and she may or may not have considered the coincidence of the date. Whatever her thoughts at the time, Minnie Bedford was on the brink of her own Lake Michigan adventure. Instead of religious fires, however, she was about to be touched by flames of an all-too-worldly nature.

Scheduled to arrive after midnight, the *Champlain* never reached the dock in Charlevoix. As the vessel rounded Fisherman's Island, within clear sight of the harbor, fire broke out in the engine room. The fire spread quickly, blocking access to the boiler and engines, which raced crazily out of control. The *Champlain*'s increasing speed created a substantial breeze, fanning the flames and turning the ship into a giant torch. Eventually, she slammed into a shoal, throwing some of the screaming passengers overboard, while others, their clothes on fire, jumped into the water to escape the inferno. The bright flames converted the *Champlain* into a gruesome sort of lighthouse, guiding fishing boats to the scene of the disaster. In all, 22 of the passengers and crew drowned or were burned to death. Among the few rescued was Minnie Bedford—burned, frightened, but very much a survivor.

Railroad at the Bottom of a Lake

In addition to the thousands of ships and boats swallowed up by Lake Michigan, railroad trains have also gone to the bottom. Trains, or parts of them, often take an economical shortcut, crossing the lake on specially designed ferries. Some, though, never reach the tracks on the other side.

In 1910 the ferry *Pere Marquette* went down, carrying with her 29 fully loaded railroad boxcars. Early on the morning of September 8, not long after leaving the terminal in Ludington, Michigan, the ferry sprang a leak. By the time a rescue ship arrived, the *Pere Marquette* was gone, railroad cars and all. Of the 62 passengers and crew, only 37 desperately splashing and sputtering survivors remained to be pulled from the water. The captain went down with his train.

On October 22, 1929, exactly one week before the great stock-market crash on Wall Street, the ferry *Milwaukee* sailed out into Lake Michigan. She was never seen or heard from again. The *Milwaukee* simply vanished. Wherever she went—presumably to the bottom of the lake—she took with her 27 heavily laden boxcars and at least 50 passengers, crew, and railroad men.

Huge lake freighters such as the *Edmund Fitzgerald* (see chapter 5) have been described by some as "floating trains." In fact, it would take at least three separate mile-long trains to carry as much iron ore as went down with the *Edmund Fitzgerald* on November 10, 1975. The *Edmund Fitzgerald* was only one of many big freighters to have plied the Great Lakes' sometimes placid waters, and she was not the first of these titanic vessels to meet with disaster. In 1958, the same year that the *Edmund Fitzgerald* was launched, the lakes lost one of their biggest and proudest ships.

Gone Like the Griffin

In November 1958 the 640-foot *Carl C. Bradley* was heading home empty, making her last run of the fall shipping season. She had left behind in Buffington, Indiana, her cargo of some 18,000 tons of limestone, enough rock to fill 300 railroad cars. As the *Bradley* approached the top of Lake Michigan, less than a day's sail from her home port of Rogers City, Michigan, she ran straight into one of the lake's proverbial November storms.

Wind whipped across the deck at upward of 70 miles per hour, and 30-foot waves slammed into the bow. But for the *Bradley*'s 35 officers and crew, all hardened veterans of furious lake tempests, confronting such ugly weather was simply part of a day's work. Despite the pitching and rolling, no one got seasick as the men wolfed down their dinner of hamburgers, French fries, and sponge cake.

Groaning under the strain placed on them by the huge waves, some of the hull plates began to shear off rivets and shoot them like bullets across the empty hold. Except for anyone unlucky enough to be caught in the line of fire, this was no particular cause for alarm. It was, in fact, a common experience in a storm. But a loud booming sound caught the attention of the entire crew just after 5:30 p.m. It was not something any of them had heard before. The boom was followed moments later by another, then another. Captain Roland Bryan and First Mate Elmer Fleming looked back from the pilothouse and, to their horror, saw the aft section of the *Bradley* begin to sag. The ship was breaking in half!

Immediately, Captain Bryan sounded a general alarm, and Fleming put out a call over the ship's radio phone to all within hearing: "Mayday! Mayday!" For the *Carl C. Bradley* and nearly all of her crew, however, it was already too late. Less than a quarter of an hour after the first sign of trouble, the *Bradley*'s bow and stern sections parted and, within minutes, went their separate ways to the bottom. Those crewmen not carried down with the ship were left to fight for their lives on the wildly tossing surface. In those brutal, 36-degree waters, it was a struggle they could not hope to win. If they could see through the storm, the lighthouse beacons calling to them from nearby Beaver Island, Cat Head, or elsewhere along the Michigan coast, it must have been a bitter reminder that safe ground was so near and yet so far away. One after another of the *Bradley's* crew either froze to death or gave up and disappeared into the dark water.

The first would-be rescue ship to arrive over the *Bradley's* watery grave was a small German freighter, the *Christian Sartori*. No survivors could be located. The *Sartori* found only an eerie scattering of wave-tossed debris. A U-boat officer in World War II, the *Sartori's* Captain Muller had witnessed such scenes in the past. He believed that all hands had been lost; but as it turned out, he was wrong. Incredibly, some fourteen hours after the big stone carrier broke in half, a Coast Guard helicopter searching the open waters of Lake Michigan spotted an orange raft. Not long afterward the crew of the cutter *Sundew* pulled aboard First Mate Fleming and Frank Mays, a young deck watchman. These two alone remained alive to tell the story of the *Carl C. Bradley's* last day on the lake.

Pier lights such as Charlevoix Pier Light (opposite page) often marked the narrow entrances of harbors or channels. This diminutive tower and beacon point the way to the harbor of Charlevoix where famed author and inveterate fisherman Ernest Hemingway spent considerable time during his youth.

Charlevoix Pier Light
Charlevoix, Michigan
1885

Among the many scenic wonders of Michigan, Lake Charlevoix is a standout. Reaching far back into the heavily forested hills of the state's wild "Hemingway" country, its pristine blue-green waters are linked to those of Lake Michigan by way of a narrow mile-long channel. Clustered along the banks of the channel are the Edwardian homes, elegant boathouses, and quaint shops of Charlevoix, a prominent early-twentieth-century resort community. A century ago, wealthy Chicago families flocked to Charlevoix to escape the summertime heat and clamor of the big city. Among those who frequented the area was the young Ernest Hemingway, who wrote some of his first stories at his father's fishing camp on nearby Walloon Lake.

Nowadays travelers come here to enjoy the natural beauty and recreational potential of the area. Motorists passing through Charlevoix on US Highway 31 will cross a drawbridge near the middle of town. To the west of the bridge is the entrance to the channel; there, a pair of concrete-and-stone piers reach out into Lake Michigan.

Near the end of the south pier stands a boxy metal tower with a small black lantern at the top. This is the modest but nonetheless fascinating Charlevoix Pier

Lighthouse. The tower dates to 1948 when it replaced an earlier skeleton structure that once stood near the end of the north pier.

At night the lantern's red light flashes every few seconds, warning vessels to stay clear of the pier. The mingling waters of the two lakes create tricky currents that rush into or out of the channel, depending on the time of day. The channel and its beacon are often used by Coast Guard vessels and recreational boaters approaching the Charlevoix harbor. They are also used by the ferries that make regular runs to Beaver Island about 25 miles to the northwest.

How to Get There
Charlevoix is a delightful coastal village just off US Highway 31 about 50 miles north of Traverse City and about 16 miles southwest of Petosky. The lighthouse is on the south side of the channel drawbridge near Grant Street. A nearby parking area provides access to the pier, the lighthouse, and an adjacent beach. For more information visit chxhistory.com.

Grand Traverse Light
North Port, Michigan
1853

Established in 1853, well before the Civil War, the Grand Traverse Lighthouse served generations of lake sailors before being decommissioned in 1972. After casting its powerful beacon out across Lake Michigan for well over a century, the old lighthouse was retired, its duties taken over by a simple skeleton structure with relatively little character. But fortunately for those of us who love historic architecture, the original buildings have been preserved and are exceptionally well maintained.

Indeed, the old lighthouse has quite a history. Intended to guide shipping into and out of Grand Traverse Bay, the lighthouse was built on Cat Head Point. Here, with its powerful fourth-order Fresnel lens, it could command the entrance to the bay. The lens beamed out toward the lake from atop a square tower and lantern room rising through the pitched roof of a large, two-story brick dwelling. Even in this isolated location, keepers and their families could live comfortably in the ample dwelling.

The station's first keeper was Philo Beers, who also served as a US deputy marshal. Apparently, the station had need of a lawman. While still under construction in 1852, it was raided by Mormon followers of a the very same King James Jesse Strang described in the introduction to this chapter. Not overly literal in their reading of the Ten Commandments, these religious raiders stole everything they could lay their hands on, including some of Beers's lighthouse equipment. Fortunately, the deputy marshal managed to drive off the king's men and save the station's all-important Fresnel lens.

Today the lighthouse is a museum filled with exhibits and mementos offering visitors a glimpse of life in a turn-of-the-twentieth-century lighthouse. Among its exhibits is the station's original Fresnel lens.

How to Get There
From Northport, North Point Road leads through exquisitely scenic Leelanau State Park to the lighthouse. The large, two-story brick dwelling is furnished with antiques, toys, and even dishes on the table, as if the keeper and his family had just stepped outside for a moment. For more information visit grandtraverselighthouse.com or call (231) 386–7195.

Point Betsie Light
Frankfort, Michigan
1858

The French called this place Pointe Aux Becs Scies, meaning "sawed beak point," but English-speaking settlers gave it a less dramatic name: Point Betsie. The government built the Point Betsie Lighthouse in 1858 to mark a key turning place for ships entering or exiting the strategic Manitou Passage. Ever since then lake sailors have considered this one of the most important lights on Lake Michigan. The original 37-foot tower and attached two-story dwelling (enlarged in 1894) still stand, and the light still burns each night.

For more than a century, Lake Michigan's often angry waters have cut away at Point Betsie, eroding the beach as if determined to reclaim the land from humanity. Its advance halted by steel breakwaters and concrete abutments, the lake has so far failed to destroy this beautiful place. That is fortunate since the Point Betsie Lighthouse now serves not just as a key navigational marker but also as a superbly educational maritime museum.

How to Get There

Located near Franklin, Michigan, just south of the popular Sleeping Bear Dunes National Lakeshore, Point Betsie Lighthouse can be reached via Michigan Highway 22 and Point Betsie Road. Station buildings house a fascinating historical museum. For more information visit pointbetsie.org or call (231) 352–7644.

Big Sable Point Light
Ludington, Michigan
1867

In 1900 the Big Sable Point tower was encased in a shell of riveted steel plates to protect it from destructive Great Lakes storms. However, the exposed bricks of the nearby Little Sable Point tower have long withstood the weather.

During its early days, Ludington, Michigan, had one of the most unusual fog signals in the country. A metal horn made in the shape of a long bugle stood beside a railroad track, and whenever a blanket of fog rolled in from the lake, a steam locomotive periodically gave a blast on its whistle. Magnified by the horn, the train whistle could be heard for many miles out on the lake.

Once the Big Sable Light was established just north of town in 1867, this clever but makeshift device gave way to a more conventional foghorn. The new lighthouse was given a 107-foot brick tower and a powerful third-order Fresnel lens so that lake sailors could be warned long before they were near enough to hear the foghorn. About the turn of the twentieth century, the tower was encased in steel plates to protect its vulnerable bricks from the harsh Lake Michigan weather.

The plates have done their job well since the tower has remained solid now for a century. Painted white, it has a broad black middle section to make it more distinctive as a daymark. Surrounded by shifting dunes, Big Sable is one of the most scenic light stations in the country.

How to Get There

The Big Sable Point Lighthouse is the primary attraction of Ludington State Park, located across the Big Sable River about six miles from Ludington. For more information visit the Sable Points Lighthouse Keepers Association at spika.org or call (231) 845–7417.

Little Sable Point Light
Silver Lake State Park, Michigan
1874

When completed in 1874, the lighthouse tower at Little Sable Point was nearly a twin of its sister at Big Sable Point near Ludington. Both towers stood 107 feet tall, both were constructed of brick, and both had a third-order Fresnel lens.

The Big Sable Point tower deteriorated and was eventually covered with steel plates, but the tower at Little Sable Point still looks much as it did more than 125 years ago. The keeper's dwelling, however, was demolished during the 1950s when the lighthouse was automated, leaving the tower to stand a solitary vigil. One of the loveliest lighthouse towers on the lakes, its red brick walls offer a handsome contrast to the white dunes and the blue water of the lake beyond.

How to Get There
The Little Sable Point Lighthouse is in Silver Lake State Park just west of Mears in Oceana County, Michigan. For more information visit the Sable Points Lighthouse Keepers Association at spika.org or call (231) 845–7417. The

spika.org website also offers helpful information on the White River Lighthouse where the station's original fourth-order Fresnel lens is on display in an attractive museum.

Pierhead Lighthouses of Lake Michigan

Many Great Lakes lighthouses are built offshore and are connected to the land by long piers or catwalks. Several fine examples of this type of lighthouse can be seen along the eastern shores of Lake Michigan. Most are located within a day's drive of one another just a few miles off US Highway 31 in western Michigan.

Among the loveliest and best known of these are a pair of pier lights located in St. Joseph, Michigan once served by one one of the earliest lighthouses on Lake Michigan. That lighthouse, built in 1832, stood on a mainland bluff. It was discontinued during the 1920s and demolished in 1955. Today the city has two lights, both located on a pier. The St. Joseph North Pier Inner and Outer Lighthouses form a range-light combination, guiding ships into the St. Joseph River channel. The pier lights seen here today date from 1907. With their distinctive shapes—the outer is cylindrical and the inner octagonal—they rank among the most beautiful man-made structures on the Great Lakes.

Likewise striking are the lighthouses that mark the entrance to the Grand River and one of the state's best deepwater harbors. Known as the Grand Haven South Pier Inner Light and the Grand Haven South Pierhead Light, they stand several hundred feet apart on a long stone pier. The inner light was built in 1895 and consists of a 51-foot steel cylinder topped by a small lantern. The squat pierhead light was originally the fog-signal building and was moved to its current location when the pier was extended in 1905. A tiny lantern nestles on the roof. The wooden structure has been sheathed in iron to protect it from Lake Michigan's destructive, storm-driven waves.

How to Get There

The St. Joseph and Grand Haven lighthouses and other beautiful pier lights depicted here and on adjacent pages are all accessible from exits off US Highway 31. For more information visit Michigan.org, swmichigan.org, or mymichiganbeach.com. A detailed map and GPS are recommended.

St. Joseph, Michigan
1832

The St. Joseph Pier Lighthouses, shown here at sunset, have been featured on a popular commemorative postage stamp.

Grand Haven, Michigan
1895

South Haven, Michigan
1903

Built in 1872, the South Haven South Pierhead Light is linked to shore by an elevated catwalk that makes access much safer during stormy weather.
MARK E. GIBSON/CORBIS DOCUMENTARY VIA GETTY IMAGES

Holland, Michigan
1936

The Holland Harbor Lighthouse wears a showy coat of red
paint which makes it easier to spot from miles out in the lake.

Muskegon, Michigan
1903

Fog settles over the striking Muskegon South Pier tower.

Michigan City East Pier Light
Michigan City, Indiana
1904

The Michigan City East Pier Lighthouse has guided ships into and out of the harbor since the early twentieth century. Built on a square concrete platform, the structure has a pyramidal roof. An octagonal tower thrusts through the roof, raising the focal plane of the light more than fifty feet above the lake. Like many similar pier lighthouses, this one is encased in steel to protect it from storms.

During the tremendous storm of November 1913, the keeper of the East Pier Lighthouse took refuge on the mainland throughout most of the heavy weather. For three days the waves pounded the pier and the lighthouse. When it was all over, about 200 feet of the elevated walkway connecting the lighthouse with the mainland had been destroyed. To enable the keeper to reach the lighthouse, engineers rigged up an aerial tram with a breeches buoy (a life preserver with a pants-like canvas seat). Keepers used this rather adventurous system for several months until the elevated walkway was repaired.

How to Get There

The Michigan City East Pier Lighthouse can be seen from many points along the shore in the somewhat confusingly named Michigan City, Indiana. In calm weather visitors often walk out on the pier to get a close-up view of the historic structure. The nearby Michigan City Lighthouse now a delightful museum, is in Washington Park off Heisman Harbor Road. The lighthouse is across from the Naval Armory building and has its own parking area. For more information visit michigancitylaporte.com or call (219) 872–5055.

The Michigan City Lighthouse has been out of service since 1904 when the nearby pier lights took over the task of guiding ships and sailors to safety. The original lighthouse now serves as a museum.

FEIFEI CUI-PAOLUZZO/MOMENT VIA GETTY IMAGES

Chicago Harbor Light
Chicago, Illinois
1832

The first Chicago lighthouse, one of the earliest on the Great Lakes, was built at the mouth of the Chicago River in 1832. As Chicago grew into one of the world's greatest cities, a series of lights, built both on the mainland and on piers in the harbor, guided a tremendous volume of shipping traffic into and out of the city. Because the St. Lawrence Seaway makes Chicago a seaport and not just a lakeport, ships from every maritime nation have docked here.

The Harbor Lighthouse seen today originally stood on the mainland at the entrance of the Chicago River, near the site of the city's first lighthouse. Built in 1893, it was given an especially fine third-order Fresnel lens, which had been intended for the Point Loma Lighthouse in California. The lens had been placed on display in that same year at Chicago's Columbian Exposition. When this now-legendary world's fair was over, lighthouse officials decided to place the lens in the recently completed Harbor Lighthouse.

In 1917, just before the United States entered World War I, the lighthouse was moved to the end of a harbor breakwater. There it has remained. Each night its historic lens throws its light out across the harbor from the lantern room atop the 48-foot brick-and-steel tower.

How to Get There
The lighthouse is closed to the public but can be seen from many points along the Chicago waterfront.

Grosse Point Light
Evanston, Illinois
1873

Among the most beautiful and storied lights on the Great Lakes, the Grosse Point Lighthouse is in many ways a superlative structure. Its second-order Fresnel is one of the most powerful lenses on the lakes, while its 113-foot tower is one of the tallest. The conical brick tower, painted yellow and trimmed in red, is exceptionally graceful.

Although it was decommissioned by the Coast Guard in 1935 and operates today as a private navigational aid, the Grosse Point Lighthouse continues to serve lake sailors just as it has since 1873. Built during the early 1870s for approximately $50,000, the station was meant to serve as a primary coastal light. It was given a double-sized keeper's dwelling and several outbuildings, which housed the fog signal and other equipment. The brick of the tower deteriorated over the years, and in 1914 the tower was encased in a layer of concrete. Today the lighthouse stands on a street lined with fine old lakefront homes. Northwestern University is nearby.

How to Get There

The lighthouse is located near the intersection of Central Street East and Sheridan Avenue in Evanston. The grounds and some station buildings are used as a combination nature and maritime center. For more information visit grossepointlighthouse.net.

Wind Point Light
Racine, Wisconsin
1880

Established in 1880, the Wind Point Lighthouse was fitted with a pair of lenses. Its third-order Fresnel lens displayed a flashing white light, while a smaller fifth-order lens marked the dangerous Racine Reef with a red light. Today the station is automated, and its Fresnel lenses have been replaced by a single airport-type beacon. The brick tower is 108 feet tall and is attached by a passageway to a two-story brick dwelling.

How to Get There
The Wind Point Lighthouse is in the Village of Wind Point south of Milwaukee. For more information visit windpointlighthouse.org or call (262) 639–3777. The Old Racine Harbor Lighthouse is closed to the public but can be seen from the pier.

North Point Light
Milwaukee, Wisconsin
1855

Milwaukee's first lighthouse, built several years before the Civil War began, served for more than 30 years before erosion threatened to topple the structure. A second tower, erected right alongside the first, was ready for service in 1888. These early towers were similar in design—octagonal in shape and made of cast iron or steel.

The 1888 tower was only 35 feet tall, and within two decades sprawling tree limbs began to obscure its beacon. Lighthouse engineers came up with a novel way to solve this problem in 1913. Rather than build a completely new light tower, they constructed a broad octagonal base that rose about 40 feet. The old tower was then lifted on top of the base, raising its overall height to 74 feet. This arrangement has served well for more than a century. The North Point beacon was decommissioned in 1994, and the station serves today as a fascinating museum.

How to Get There
The lighthouse is in Lake Park, just off Wahl Avenue in Milwaukee. For more information visit northpointlighthouse.org or call (414) 332–6754.

Rawley Point Light
Two Rivers, Wisconsin
1854

The waters around Rawley Point just north of Two Rivers, Wisconsin, are deceptively tranquil. Not far from shore a deadly shoal lurks just beneath the surface of Lake Michigan waiting to rip open the hull of any vessel that strays too near. After several tragic nineteenth-century wrecks, a light was finally placed on the point to warn ships against the danger. Completed in 1854, it guided mariners with a modest beacon that beamed from a small tower and lantern perched on the roof of the keeper's dwelling.

In 1894 this light was replaced by the soaring metal tower that still guards Rawley Point today. More than 110 feet tall, the present tower is a steel skeleton structure with a central cylinder braced by eight legs. At the top is a three-level lantern complex equipped with an unusually powerful aero-marine beacon. Its light can be seen from 28 miles away.

How to Get There

The tower and adjacent multistory dwelling, now a Coast Guard residence, are closed to the public, but respectful visitors are welcome to walk the grounds. The station is surrounded by lush Point Beach State Park, which offers camping, picnicking, hiking, and a wonderful opportunity to view the lighthouse. Located off Sandy Bay Road, the park and lighthouse are a short distance from nearby Two Rivers, Wisconsin.

Lighthouses of Door County

During the 1860s, while the nation's attention was focused on the Civil War, shipping increased dramatically on Lake Michigan, especially along the 250-mile shoreline of Wisconsin's Door County. Native American peoples called this land "Death's Door" because of the tricky currents and dangerous reefs that claimed the lives of so many braves who paddled their canoes through the treacherous channels into long, narrow Green Bay. European settlers who flocked here during the nineteenth century took a less foreboding view of the place and shortened the name to "Door." Not long after the influx of immigrants began, the government started building lighthouses here to make the channels less threatening.

Among the earliest navigational markers established on the long, dagger-shaped peninsula that forms Green Bay was the Eagle Bluff Lighthouse. Marking a safe channel from Lake Michigan into Green Bay, its light first shined in 1868, the same year that Ulysses S. Grant was elected president. Its square, 43-foot brick tower was set at a diagonal into the side of the one-and-a-half-story dwelling, which made it easier for keepers to reach the tower when cold winds blew in off the lake. Ironically, there has been no keeper here since 1909 as the Eagle Bluff Lighthouse was among the first in America to be automated. Still active, the old lighthouse has done its work alone for nearly a century.

Another prominent Door County light tower rises from Cana Island just off the Lake Michigan shore of Door County. Established in 1870, the light marks the northern approaches to Baileys Harbor. To make sure that the 86-foot tower and adjacent one-and-a-half-story dwelling could withstand the lake's prodigious storms, construction crews built the structures with brick, in this case a light-colored variety. But just as a yellow-brick road may lead to an uncertain future, so too with yellow-brick lighthouses. Within just a few decades, the brick showed signs of severe weathering, and the tower seemed in danger of crumbling. To protect it, the Lighthouse Board had the tower encased in a cocoonlike shell made of individual metal plates riveted together. A low, white-stone causeway connects Cana Island to the mainland.

To guide ships along the stretch of Lake Michigan nearest to Baileys Harbor, the Lighthouse Board established a pair of range lights here in 1870. These lights replaced a much older, single-lens lighthouse located on a small island far out in the harbor. Range lights mark shipping channels by displaying not one but at least two lights, arrayed one behind the other. When viewed from midchannel, the lights appear one atop the other and perpendicular to the surface of the water. If the lights begin to tilt to the right or left, a pilot knows that his ship may be straying dangerously out of the channel.

At Baileys Harbor the lower, or front-range, light was housed in a squat, 21-foot wooden tower down beside the lake. The upper, or rear-range, light shined from a gabled tower atop a clapboard dwelling some 1,000 feet inland. The station was automated in 1930 and afterward was cared for by Lutheran ministers, who used the dwelling as a parsonage right up until the lights were discontinued during the 1960s.

Door County offers at least a dozen other wonderful lighthouses, most of them still active. Besides those described above, visitors can see and enjoy the Sturgeon Bay Ship Canal Light and North Pierhead Light, Potawatomi Lighthouse on Rock Island, Plum Island Range Light, Pilot Island Lighthouse, Chambers Island Lighthouse, Sherwood Point Lighthouse, and several lesser beacons. Each of these historic lights has unique and interesting features, and each is well worth a visit

How to Get There
Most travelers reach Door County from Green Bay and other points south via Wisconsin Highway 42 or 57. Visitors should stop first in Sturgeon Bay at the Door County Maritime Museum, located adjacent to Sunset Park at the foot of Florida Street. For information on the museum visit dcmm.org or call (920) 743–5958. For more information on Door County visit doorcounty.com.

Eagle Bluff, Wisconsin
1868

Still active, the Eagle Bluff Lighthouse guides ships entering Green Bay from Lake Michigan. Note that the square tower and attached dwelling were constructed from the same yellow brick.

Cana Island, Wisconsin
1870

The Cana Island Lighthouse tower and attached dwelling were built in 1870 using the same dark yellow brick. Damaged by weather, the tower was later encased in a shell of riveted steel plates to protect it from Lake Michigan storms. JAMESBREY/E+ VIA GETTY IMAGES

Baileys Harbor, Wisconsin
1870

The Old Bailey's Harbor Lighthouse could be mistaken for a schoolhouse or a church. In fact, it once served as a Lutheran parsonage.

Sturgeon Bay, Wisconsin
1903

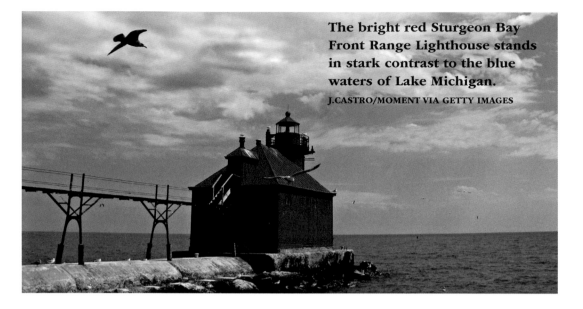

The bright red Sturgeon Bay Front Range Lighthouse stands in stark contrast to the blue waters of Lake Michigan.

J.CASTRO/MOMENT VIA GETTY IMAGES

Sherwood Point, Wisconsin
1883

The Sherwood Point Lighthouse marks the western entrance to the Sturgeon Bay Ship Canal. This was the last light station on the Great Lakes to be automated.

Seul Choix Point Light
Gulliver, Michigan
1895

Early French explorers found out the hard way that there were very few places to take shelter from a storm in this part of Lake Michigan. The harbor at Seul Choix was one such welcome refuge, which is why they gave it a name meaning "only choice." Despite its inviting harbor, Seul Choix Point did not receive a lighthouse until late in the nineteenth century. Congress finally appropriated the money for the project in 1886, but, partly because of its remote location, the lighthouse was not completed and fully operational until 1895.

The conical brick tower, 78 feet tall, was topped by a ten-sided, cast-iron lantern, giving its third-order Fresnel lens a focal plane just over 80 feet above the lake. When the Coast Guard automated the lighthouse, the Fresnel lens was removed and replaced by an airport-style beacon, visible from about 17 miles out in the lake.

The two-story brick keeper's dwelling still stands and is attached to the tower by an enclosed brick passageway. Although the structures and the grounds are now the property of the state of Michigan, this is still an operating light station. Neither the tower nor the dwelling is open to the public.

How to Get There
The Seul Choix Point Lighthouse is located near Gulliver off US Highway 2 on the Michigan Upper Peninsula. For more information visit the Gulliver Historical Society at greatlakelighthouse.com or call (906) 283–3183.

Part Five

ROMANTIC BEACONS OF THE LEVIATHAN LAKE

Superior

Known to Native Americans as Gitche Gumee and to most others as Superior, it is the Earth's greatest freshwater lake. More than 350 miles long, 160 miles wide, and a quarter mile deep, it covers 31,200 square miles of the continental heartland in a cold, dark blanket of blue water. A liquid highway for ore, grain, and chemical freighters, container ships, and other vessels of every description, it is one of the most heavily traveled bodies of water on the planet, and yet its shores include some of the most isolated spots in North America.

Ten percent of the Earth's fresh water is locked up in this one huge lake. With the addition of a little salt, Lake Superior could be listed among the world's seas. Even without the salt, Superior is a mammoth body of water deserving and receiving the highest measure of respect from mariners and landlubbers alike. Ringed by dozens of grand navigational lights, the big lake is a lighthouse lover's dream, but for the keepers of the lake's many lighthouses it was anything but a paradise.

The hardy men and women who once served as keepers at one or another of Lake Superior's remote outposts—places like Split Rock, the Apostle Islands, the Rock of Ages, Passage Island, Seul Choix, and Au Sable—were surely among the loneliest people in America, and the toughest. Usually located at water's edge, lighthouses and their keepers are often no less exposed to heavy weather than the ships and sailors they serve. But unlike ships, lighthouses cannot move, cannot run for safe harbor, cannot remain tied up at the dock until the worst is over. In a storm they must stand their ground and take their beating, and so must their keepers. But no more.

During the 1960s and 1970s, the Coast Guard automated the last manned lighthouses on the Great Lakes, including those on Superior. Afterward, their lamps and mechanisms operated by computers, photosensitive cells, and other "electronic keepers," the lake lighthouses continued their vigil alone. In the past, however, their work had always required the help of human hands.

Life on the Rocks

It is easy to imagine that lighthouse keepers were hermits, fugitives from noisy city streets and crowded factories who preferred a simpler, more peaceful life at water's edge. Generally speaking, however, that was not the case. Mostly they were ordinary Americans glad of the steady work and regular pay.

Keepers' salaries never amounted to much—often no more than 50 dollars per month, and much less than that during the nineteenth century; but almost by definition, the job came with a house and an excellent view. Remote light stations were supplied with food, delivered every few months by government lighthouse tenders, and usually there was a plot of ground where the keepers could grow vegetables and raise a few chickens. Many keepers lived with their families; some stations, though, such as the Rock of Ages Lighthouse, were much too isolated or too dangerous for family life.

Looking something like an enormous spark plug, the Rock of Ages Lighthouse rises from the open waters of Lake Superior about five miles off Isle Royale, itself one of the nation's most remote places. Nowadays, like all other Great Lakes lighthouses, the Rock of Ages Light is automated. But from 1908, the year it went into service, until the last resident crew left the station in 1977, the light was operated by a keeper and three assistants, who would remain on the Rock for up to eight months at a time. They arrived at the station in April and were taken ashore again in early December when the thickening ice forced shipping off the lakes. The denizens of the Rock were allowed occasional shore leave on Isle Royale, but otherwise they lived at the station full-time. In heavy weather no one could approach the station or leave it. If radio communication went down, the station crew could be cut off from all contact with the outside world.

Utterly barren, the Rock itself was only about 50 feet wide and supported not a single bush or blade of grass. Inside the 130-foot steel-plated tower, a spiral staircase offered access to a few small bunk rooms where the keepers slept; a galley and dining area where they ate; storage and equipment rooms where they worked; and, of course, the lantern room, with its huge second-order Fresnel lens. For the most part this was the keepers' whole world.

In 1931, in the middle of the Great Depression, a young Detroit reporter named Stella Champney sailed with the tender *Marigold* as it made its semiannual visits to Lake Superior lighthouses. At the Rock of Ages Lighthouse, she interviewed first assistant keeper C. A. McKay.

McKay had had a terrifying experience only the year before. As a storm brewed out on the lake, his boss, keeper Emil Mueller, had fallen from the tower's spiral staircase and landed squarely on the bed where McKay was sleeping. McKay was uninjured, but Mueller lay dead of a heart attack.

McKay's explanation for the tragic incident was a simple one: "Too many steps. One room on top of another clear to the top. His heart gave out."

What was it like being out here in a storm?

"You can't see anything but water," said McKay. "You can't hear anything but its roar. See that pier around the tower? It looks pretty high up and safe. Well, in a real storm, heavy, green water sweeps over it. You can't even see it sometimes. You can't get away from the water even at the top of the tower. Spray sweeps over the tower windows and, when it's very cold, freezes on the glass. You can't hear anything but the boom! boom! boom! of the seas as they sweep over the rocks, or the crack like gunfire as they hit the tower."

What about the food? McKay and some of the other men at the station complained of having to do their own cooking. "Ever hear about the time that four men nearly starved to death out here?" asked McKay. "The tender was a week late. They had a can of tomatoes left and no tender in sight. So they piled into the lighthouse motorboat and went to the Canadian shore, more than 20 miles away, leaving a note for the skipper. He beat 'em to Duluth by two days at that. They had to hunt farmhouses for food before they could work their way back to civilization."

Was it lonely living on the Rock? "You can't guess the half of it," said McKay. "No where to go on shore leave but Isle Royale. Ha! Ha!"

The Mermaid's Song

The loneliness could have quite an impact on the keepers, especially those who lived without their families. Stella Champney spoke also to Passage Island keeper James Gagnon. "Live around these isolated lighthouse stations long enough and you'll be seeing mermaids," said Gagnon, "like John Whelan down at Sand Hills [Lighthouse]. He says he sees mermaids on the rocks and hears them singing." Gagnon may have thought Whelan's mermaid sightings were funny, but he was quick to add that "I'm going to hunt mermaids on Passage Island myself this summer."

Champney knew the keepers endured their loneliness and hardship for a reason. The Great Lakes—indeed, all navigable waters—are dangerous. The lights and foghorns faithfully maintained by these men, and no few women, were absolutely essential for safe navigation on stormy Lake Superior.

Not long after leaving the Rock of Ages Lighthouse, Captain Gunwald Gundersen gave Champney a graphic illustration of the lake's dangers to shipping.

"That's the wreck of the Booth Fisheries steamer *America*," Gundersen said, pointing to a ghostly bow rising from the shimmering waters off Isle Royale. "She struck a rock early one morning in the summer of 1928. She hangs over a cliff and salvage is impossible.

"I'll show you how it happened. See the perfect reflection of the trees on the water? The captain of the ship was asleep and a new mate was taking her out of the harbor. Captains must get some sleep, you know. The mate mistook the reflection on the water for land and made a miscalculation that threw him off course. The boat struck and there she lies yet. Some day she will slip off the reef and disappear forever."

Captain Gundersen assured Champney that the *America*'s "crew and the passengers got safely to shore and were taken to a hotel on Isle Royale." Both Gundersen and his guest understood, however, that many wrecks on the Great Lakes end more tragically. Less than 20 years earlier, the monster storm of November 1913 had slammed into the lakes, exacting a ghoulish toll in ships and lives. No doubt both the experienced tender captain and the young journalist who stood beside him on the bridge of the *Marigold* were all too familiar with this and many other shipping disasters on the lakes. It is easy to imagine that, as they sailed past the bow of the ruined *America*, they held their breath in a shared moment of silence.

WBRITTEN/E+ VIA GETTY IMAGES

Point Iroquois Light
Brimley, Michigan
1855

Ships headed for the St. Marys River near Sault Ste. Marie face a pair of dangers. On their port side are the reefs near Gros Cap in Canada, while on the starboard side are the ship-killing rocks off Point Iroquois. The St. Marys became a heavily trafficked thoroughfare after the Soo Locks connected Superior to the other lakes in 1855, and since that time many vessels have been lost while approaching the river. Often an otherwise minor navigational error can be fatal here.

To help captains enter the St. Marys safely, a small lighthouse was built on Iroquois Point not long after the Soo Locks opened. Fitted with a sixth-order Fresnel lens, this modest wood tower served until 1871, when it was replaced by the impressive 65-foot brick tower and dwelling that still stand on the point today. The lighthouse served for nearly a century before the Coast Guard discontinued it in 1965.

Point Iroquois gets its name from a massacre that took place here in 1662. A war party sent westward by the Iroquois Confederation was set upon and slaughtered by an army of Ojibwa.

How to Get There
From Brimley, Six Mile Road and Lakeshore Drive lead to the lighthouse which is open to the public during warm weather months. For more information visit saultste marie.com or call (906) 632–3366.

Whitefish Point Light
Whitefish Point, Michigan
1848

In summer, visitors flock to the Whitefish Point Lighthouse and the adjacent shipwreck museum. The famed ore freighter *Edmund Fitzgerald* was lost near here to a powerful "Witch of November" storm during the 1970s.

The southeastern reaches of Lake Superior have long been known as a graveyard for ships. Hundreds of vessels, including the famed *Edmund Fitzgerald*, lie on the cold, deep bottom here where the lake approaches Whitefish Bay. The loss of so many ships in this area is made more mysterious by the fact that the bay itself is relatively calm. Seemingly, even in the worst of storms, the ships and their crews need only round Whitefish Point to reach safety. But all too often they have failed to do either.

The very first ship known to sail on Superior, the 60-foot trading vessel *Invincible*, perished in gale-force winds and towering waves near here in 1816. Many other vessels have suffered the same fate. Some were big, well-known ships such as the *Edmund Fitzgerald*, and their destruction made headlines across the country. Many others were lesser vessels, but their loss was nonetheless tragic.

In 1915 the 186-foot lumber freighter *Myron* foundered in a blizzard off Whitefish Point. The weight of the ice building up on the hull and deck dragged the freighter farther and farther down into the waves until water, pouring into the holds, snuffed out the fires in the boiler room. With no power, the little ship was doomed. The crew managed to scramble into lifeboats, but the water around the ship was filled with tons of lumber that had washed overboard. Thrown about like battering rams by the waves, the heavy lumber crushed the lifeboats and the men in them. The keeper and his family at Whitefish Point Light Station could hear the prayers and screams of the sailors as they died but could do nothing to help. Ironically, the captain, who had elected to go down with his ship, survived by clinging to a piece of the shattered pilothouse until it washed up on the beach.

When the November winds blow on Lake Superior, the most welcome sight a sailor is likely to see is the beacon from the Whitefish Point Lighthouse. This light has shined onto the big lake more-or-less unfailingly—except for the night when the *Edmund Fitzgerald* went down—for more than 150 years. To many lake sailors, the light is more than a navigational marker—it is a welcoming call from home.

The Whitefish Point Lighthouse is a remarkable structure. A steel cylinder some 80 feet tall, it is supported by a skeletal steel framework. Its modern, functional appearance is all the more extraordinary when one considers that it was built in 1861, during Abraham Lincoln's first year in the White House. Lighthouse engineers were experimenting with skeletal structures at that time. The design is intended to take stress off the building during high winds.

Appropriately, the dwelling now houses the Great Lakes Shipwreck Museum. Here visitors with open eyes and active imaginations can step back in time and relive the last moments aboard the *Edmund Fitzgerald* and many other ill-fated ships claimed forever by the lakes.

How to Get There
One of America's most fabled light stations, the Whitefish Point Lighthouse can be reached from Mackinac Bridge by taking I-75 north to Michigan Highway 123 and Paradise. From Paradise, Wire Road leads to the point and the lighthouse. An additional attraction is the Great Lakes Shipwreck Museum, where the haunting world of shipwrecks can be explored. For more information visit shipwreckmuseum.com or call (888) 492–3747.

Crisp Point Light
West of Paradise, Michigan
1904

Few coasts anywhere in the world are more treacherous than the southeastern shores of Lake Superior. Hundreds of notable vessels have been lost in this graveyard of ships, and the ribs of more than a few can still be seen lying in its sandy shallows. Particularly dangerous is Crisp Point, about 14 miles from the key navigational station at Whitefish Point, where lake freighters leave the shelter of Whitefish Bay to brave the open waters of Superior. Vessels straying too near the shore became ensnared in a line of deadly shoals reaching out from Crisp Point.

In 1904 a stout light tower was built on Crisp Point to accompany an existing lifesaving station. The new navigational station was given a two-story, brick keeper's residence, a 58-foot brick tower, and a fourth-order Fresnel lens, which displayed a red light.

The facility had to be supplied almost entirely by boat. Located far from any major town and with no serviceable road to link it with even the most remote Upper Peninsula communities, Crisp Point was among the most isolated light stations in America. Not surprisingly, it was not a favorite duty station for Lighthouse Service keepers.

The lifesaving station at Crisp Point was closed up during the 1930s, and some years later the light was automated. After that no one lived at Crisp Point, and the station began to deteriorate. The Coast Guard destroyed most of the buildings here in 1965 but left the tower and its light in place. The light was finally deactivated in 1989. The abandoned lighthouse might have fallen prey to wind, weather, and the steadily advancing waters of Lake Superior. However, the historic structure has been saved and lovingly restored thanks to donations by generous individuals and groups, including the American Lighthouse Foundation and two local Native American tribes. The Crisp Point Light was restored to service in 2013.

How to Get There
Located far off the beaten path, the Crisp Point Lighthouse can only be reached from Paradise via Michigan Highway 123 and County Road 412 which can be muddy and difficult to follow. For more information visit crisppointlighthouse.org.

The Crisp Point Lighthouse (opposite page) brightens a barren stretch of Lake Superior shoreline west of Whitefish Point. Although deactivated in 1989, the historic lighthouse returned to service 1989.

Au Sable Point Light
Grand Marais, Michigan
1874

KENNETH KEIFER/500PX PLUS VIA GETTY IMAGES

For many years sailors dreaded the 80 miles of dark shoreline stretching eastward from Grand Island Lighthouse to the famed light on Whitefish Point. Unmarked by any navigational light, these dangerous shores claimed dozens of ships. To fill the gap and save lives, a lighthouse was placed on Au Sable Point in 1874.

An 87-foot brick tower was built on a rise, placing the light about 107 feet above the lake's surface. Its third-order Fresnel lens displayed a fixed white light. The attached, two-story brick keeper's dwelling was spacious, but those who lived in it knew theirs was one of the most remote mainland light stations in America. The nearest town, Grand Marais, was more than a dozen miles away, and there was no all-season road. Keepers either hiked in or came by boat.

Perhaps because of its isolation, the Coast Guard automated the light in 1958, turning the property and buildings over to the National Park Service for inclusion in Pictured Rocks National Lakeshore. Although the light remains active, the old Fresnel lens has been removed and placed in the Nautical and Maritime Museum in Grand Marais.

Pictured Rocks National Lakeshore encompasses a remarkable variety of attractions, including Munising Falls, Miners Castle (a nine-story-tall monolith), trails, streams, woodlands, beaches, and, of course, Au Sable Light Station. Twelve miles of beach offer solitude and nearly endless barefoot walks over white sand and pebbles. Grand Sable Dunes cannot match the Sahara for sheer size, but its four-square miles of shifting sand are enough to impress.

How to Get There

Just as its keepers once did, visitors must walk to this lighthouse in Pictured Rocks National Lakeshore on the Upper Peninsula. The tower is a considerable distance via gravel road and trail from the park headquarters in Grand Marais. For more information visit the national lakeshore website at nps.gov/piro or call (906) 387–3700.

Munising Range Lights
Munising, Michigan
1908

A pair of rather extraordinary range lights mark the harbor at Munising on Michigan's Upper Peninsula. Enclosed on three sides by thick forest, the squat rear-range light (below, left) may remind a fanciful visitor of the tin woodsman in The Wizard of Oz. The more traditional front-range light (below, right) is a 50-foot steel cylinder. What sets it apart is the fact that it is much taller than its rear-range partner. Usually, the opposite is true.

Both the range-light towers at Munising were built in 1908 to guide vessels along a narrow safe channel through Munising Bay. Interestingly, the rear-range light was fitted with a locomotive headlamp rather than a standard lighthouse lens. Both lights remain in operation.

How to Get There
Munising can be reached from Sault Ste. Marie or Marquette via Michigan Highway 28. The Munising Front Range Light is just west of town on the right side of the highway. The rear light can be found a few blocks away at the far end of Hemlock Street.

DANITA DELIMONT/GALLO IMAGES ROOTS
RF COLLECTION VIA GETTY IMAGES

Marquette Harbor Light
Marquette, Michigan
1853

With the discovery of copper in the mountains of Michigan's Upper Peninsula in the 1840s, and iron later in the century, Marquette became an important port. A lighthouse built here in 1853 guided ore freighters and other vessels into and out of the city's harbor. With its poor-quality construction, however, it held out only a few years against Lake Superior's hard winters.

The square, masonry tower that replaced it in 1866 proved much more durable and still serves the city and its harbor today. The lantern atop the 40-foot attached tower once held a classic fourth-order Fresnel lens, but an automated beacon has taken its place.

With its red brick walls poised at the summit of a rocky headland, the Marquette Harbor Lighthouse is quite scenic, and residents of this hardworking town are justifiably proud of it. The lighthouse and its surroundings present photographers with an irresistible subject, especially in the fall when the nearby hills are cloaked in color.

How to Get There

The harbor lighthouse can be reached by following Lake Street off US Highway 41 in Marquette. Part of an active U.S. Coast Guard station, the lighthouse is off-limits to the public. However, an excellent view can be had from a parking area at the Marquette Maritime Museum on Lakeshore Drive. The museum itself has much to offer. For more information visit mqtmaritimemuseum.com or call (906) 226–2006.

Eagle Harbor Light
Eagle Harbor, Michigan
1851

Winters on Michigan's Upper Peninsula are notoriously severe. But the weather did not deter the rapid development of mining when deposits of copper and iron were found in the nineteenth century. The richest veins of copper were located on the Keweenaw Peninsula, which thrusts out to the northeast toward the center of Lake Superior. Ship traffic into Eagle Harbor and nearby Copper Harbor expanded rapidly to carry the copper bounty to markets in the East. As a result, government officials soon saw the need for lighthouses to guide the ore freighters.

The Eagle Harbor Lighthouse began operation in 1851. During its first few years of service, it was equipped with an old-style lamp and reflector, but this outdated system was replaced by a Fresnel lens in 1857. Lake Superior weather took a heavy toll on the light-station buildings, and by 1870 they had to be replaced. The 44-foot, octagonal brick tower and attached dwelling seen at Eagle Harbor today date from 1871. For many years the tower held a fourth-order Fresnel lens, but in 1968 it was removed in favor of an airport-style beacon. The station has been automated since 1971.

How to Get There
Most Keweenah Peninsula visitors follow US Highway 41 which, interestingly, links often frigid Lake Superior with far-off balmy Florida. Eagle Harbor and its lighthouse are located only a few miles from that fabled highway's northernmost extremity. Extraordinarily picturesque, the tower and its fog signal building house a maritime museum open from mid-June through October. For more information visit keweenaw history.org.

Lighthouses of the Apostle Islands

As anyone who has seen them is likely to agree, the Apostle Islands, off Wisconsin's Chequamegon Peninsula, are a national treasure. Fortunately, Congress has recognized their unique aesthetic value and has set aside 21 of the 22 islands by making them part of the Apostle Islands National Lakeshore.

Every summer visitors flock to the Apostles to enjoy their natural beauty, wildlife, and pristine beaches. But the islands offer another extraordinary attraction as well. Strung in a semicircle around the island chain is a jeweled necklace of five lighthouses, all of them more than a century old and in excellent condition. Well maintained by National Park Service personnel, these venerable structures make the Apostle Islands National Lakeshore something of an outdoor lighthouse museum.

Built in 1857, Michigan Island Lighthouse is the oldest in the Apostles. Like many early lights in the Upper Midwest, this one went into service not long after the Soo

---

Michigan Island Light
1857

In 1930 the U.S. Coast Guard deactivated the old Michigan Island Lighthouse, replacing it with this 102-foot skeleton tower moved from Schooner Ledge in Maine, where it had served since 1869.

Locks opened Lake Superior to shipping from the other lakes. The whitewashed stucco tower with its dwelling suggests a New England coastal lighthouse. The light guided ships along the eastern side of the Apostles for more than 70 years before its duties were taken over in 1930 by a skeleton-style light tower moved here from Maine. Still in operation today, the latter structure consists of a cylindrical metal tower supported by a framework of steel.

One of the oddities of the Michigan Island Lighthouse is the fact that it was built in the wrong place. The station was originally intended for nearby Long Island. No one knows who made the mistake, or why. In 1858 a second lighthouse was built on the correct site—La Pointe on Long Island. A simple wooden-frame structure, it served until 1895, when it was replaced by a steel tower similar to the one later seen on Michigan Island. In 1964 its fourth-order Fresnel lens gave way to an airport-style beacon displaying a flashing green light.

The Raspberry Island Lighthouse dates to the Civil War. Built on a high bank, the wooden-frame tower and keeper's dwelling were completed in 1863. For almost a

Raspberry Island Light
1863

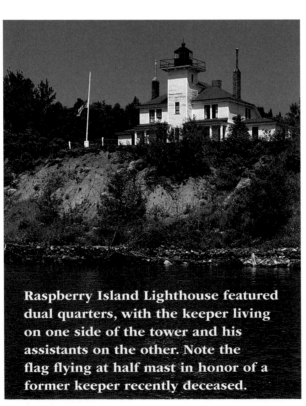

Raspberry Island Lighthouse featured dual quarters, with the keeper living on one side of the tower and his assistants on the other. Note the flag flying at half mast in honor of a former keeper recently deceased.

century its fifth-order lens shined from the lantern room in the 40-foot tower. Then, in 1957, the Coast Guard removed the light and mounted it on a pole in front of the fog-signal building.

For more than 125 years, ships have been guided around the Apostles by the Outer Island Lighthouse, in service since 1874. A traditional conical brick tower, some 80 feet tall, it stands on a high bank, raising the focal plane of its light more than 130 feet above the lake's surface. The lantern once held a third-order Fresnel lens, but nowadays it employs a plastic lens displaying a flashing white light.

Outer Island Light
1874

Ships attempting to circumnavigate the Apostles have looked to the Outer Island Lighthouse for guidance since 1874.

On the west side of the Apostles, Sand Island Lighthouse guided ships for half a century—from 1881 to 1931—before it, too, was replaced by a steel skeleton tower. The original brownstone structure was leased afterward as a private residence, and it has survived the years since then intact.

Devils Island has little in common with the infamous French penal colony of the same name. Keepers lived quite comfortably here in the light station's spacious Queen Anne–style brick dwelling. The station was so well-appointed, in fact, that it attracted a visit from President and Mrs. Calvin Coolidge in August 1928. Accompanied by a party of about fifty well-wishers, the fun-loving Coolidges enjoyed a sumptuous lunch on the station dock. Such events were rare, however, to say the least.

Sand Island Light
1881

A young summer visitor graces a lush field against the backdrop of the historic Sand Island stone tower and dwelling.

The work here was hard and demanded an extraordinary variety of skills—even the ability to handle a dog team. The winter of 1924–1925 closed in so fast that a gas-powered buoy had to be abandoned in Chequamegon Bay, just east of the Apostles. Before leaving his station for the season, a keeper drove a dogsled out over the solidly frozen lake, shut off the gas, and retrieved the buoy's valuable lantern.

Such heroics on the part of lighthouse keepers (not to mention dogs) are no longer seen in the Apostles. Devils Island Lighthouse, placed in operation in 1891, was the last of the Apostle Island lights to be automated in 1978. Its flashing red warning becomes a flashing white light during winter for shipping traffic loaded with lumber, iron ore, and stone. The last station to be automated, in 1978, it is part of the protective ring of lights built by the U.S. Lighthouse Service to guide ships safely around the hazardous Apostle Islands.

Devils Island Light
1891

This 82-foot tower marks Devils Island on the northwestern side of the Apostle's chain. Its flashing red warning beacon becomes a flashing white light during winter for shipping traffic loaded with lumber, iron ore, and stone.

How to Get There

Apostle Islands visitors should stop first at the National Lakeshore Visitor Center in the old county courthouse in Bayfield. For more information on the Apostles and their lighthouses, visit the lakeshore website at nps.gov/apis or call (715) 779-3397

Duluth Breakwater Lights
Duluth, Minnesota
1901

At the far western end of Lake Superior is Duluth, Minnesota, a hardworking city famous for having provided much of the iron ore fed into the Bessemer furnaces of America's steel mills. Mountains of ore have been loaded here into long Great Lakes freighters for the trip to the Soo Locks and beyond. Today, in addition to freighters, the Duluth lakefront is attracting throngs of tourists.

Located on one of the nation's busiest industrial waterfronts, Canal Park offers plenty for visitors to see and enjoy. In addition to the heavily trafficked ship canal, the extraordinary Aerial Bridge, and a fine maritime museum, there are three delightful lighthouses, each with its own still-operational Fresnel lens.

Built just after the turn of the twentieth century, the lighthouses are located on breakwaters alongside the channel connecting the inner harbor to Lake Superior. A lighthouse was placed beside the channel as early as 1870; but in 1901 it was replaced by a pair of light towers, one at either end of the breakwater. The South Breakwater Outer Lighthouse consists of a 35-foot tower rising from the corner of a squat brick fog-signal building. Its fourth-order Fresnel lens was imported from France. Erected at the same time was the South Breakwater Inner Lighthouse, a steel cylinder-type tower with a supporting skeleton frame. This lighthouse, somewhat shorter than its seaward brother, displays a flashing light produced by a fourth-order bull's-eye Fresnel lens.

The Duluth North Breakwater Lighthouse went into service during the spring of 1910. Its metal frame is enclosed by riveted steel plates. The lantern atop its 37-foot tower contains a fifth-order Fresnel lens.

How to Get There

The Duluth Breakwater Lights are among the key attractions of the increasingly popular Canal Park and waterfront area not far from downtown Duluth. The lighthouses are on piers beside the commercially vital ship canal. Nearby is the Lake Superior Maritime Visitors Center operated by the Army Corps of Engineers. For more information visit lsmma.com or call (218) 727–2497.

With its hardy, industrial reputation, one might expect Duluth's lighthouses to be hardworking rather than bucolic and that is, indeed, the case. These mark the busy channel leading to the city's industrial waterfront.

THEODORE SADLER/MOMENT VIA GETTY IMAGES

Two Harbors Light
Two Harbors, Minnesota
1892

Anyone seeking an authentic but comfortable experience in a lighthouse B&B need look no further than the Two Harbors Lighthouse northeast of Duluth. Dating to 1891, this is the oldest lighthouse in Minnesota.

Looking very much like an early-twentieth-century elementary school, the Two Harbors Lighthouse is not as well known as the much photographed and celebrated Split Rock Lighthouse, about 20 miles to the north. This redbrick, can-do navigational marker remains active, however, whereas its more famous neighbor is now a museum. Built in 1892 to guide iron freighters and other ships to the busy loading docks nearby, the Two Harbors Light continues to do the same job today.

Emanating from a 50-foot square tower set into the southwest corner of the dwelling, its light has been a familiar sight to generations of lake pilots and navigators. The lighthouse sits on a grassy knoll, boosting the focal plane of the light to nearly 80 feet above the surface of the lake. The lantern room once contained a fourth-order Fresnel lens, but it was replaced with a matched pair of airport-style beacons in 1970. The Coast Guard completed automation of the lighthouse in 1981, and in 1986 it turned the building over to the Lake County Historical Society for use as a museum. In 2001 the Society also assumed responsibility for maintaining the beacon.

How to Get There

A parking area off Third Street in Two Harbors provides access to the lighthouse. The Lake County Historical Society operates the historic combination residence and tower as a lighthouse as a bed and breakfast offering visitors a chance to spend the night in a functioning lighthouse. For more information visit lakecountyhistoricalsociety.org or call (218) 834–4898.

Split Rock Lighthouse
Two Harbors, Minnesota
1910

Compasses do not always read true in western Lake Superior. Captains steaming toward Duluth are used to seeing their compass needles swing this way and that as if the Earth's magnetic poles had decided to take a holiday. The problem is iron—mountains of it—ashore and lesser mountains in the holds of passing ships. In these parts sailors are particularly thankful for lighthouses and other navigational aids.

High up on a Minnesota cliff overlooking Lake Superior stands one of the world's great lighthouses. Photographed literally millions of times, framed in countless post-cards, and featured on the covers of hundreds of publications, it is certainly one of America's best-known and most visited lighthouse.

Ironically, Minnesota's Split Rock Lighthouse is no longer an official Coast Guard light station. But that does not deter the visitors who swarm here every day during the summer to enjoy this magnificent lighthouse and the spectacular view from its high, stony perch.

An octagonal yellow-brick structure, the tower is only 54 feet high, but the cliff beneath it soars more than 120 feet over the lake. This places the focal plane of the light 168 feet above the lake level and makes Split Rock one of the loftiest lighthouses on the Great Lakes.

Built in 1910, the lighthouse owes its existence in part to a hurricane-like November blizzard that tore across Superior five years earlier. The great storm of 1905 caught dozens of ore boats and freighters out on the lake. More than 30 were driven onto rocks and crushed. Several disappeared forever into the lake's extreme depths. One, the 430-foot *Mataafa*, met her end within sight of Duluth Harbor. Another, the *William Edenborn*, was flung ashore and torn apart on Split Rock itself. Dozens of lives were lost in the storm.

This calamity convinced lighthouse officials that navigational aids on Lake Superior must be improved. The most important step they took to accomplish the upgrading was construction of a light station at Split Rock, which would no easy task. Building the lighthouse proved a difficult and expensive task. By the time the tower, lantern, fog-signal building, and detached dwellings were completed and the lamps ready to be lit during the summer of 1910, the project had cost taxpayers more than $72,000.

The station's flashing light was produced by a bivalve-style Fresnel lens that looked something like a huge glass clamshell. For many years light for the beacon came from an oil vapor lamp; but after electricity reached the station in 1939, a 1,000-watt bulb was placed inside the lens. The light flashed once every ten seconds and could be seen from 22 miles out on the lake.

The Coast Guard decommissioned the lighthouse in 1969, handing it over to the state of Minnesota for use as a park. More than 200,000 visitors enjoy the lighthouse and surrounding 100-acre park each year. There are several fine trails, and a variety of films and exhibits illuminate the station and its history.

How to Get There

Most travelers reach Split Rock from Duluth or Two Harbors via US Highway 61, otherwise known as the North Shore Highway. Split Rock is now a Minnesota state park, and in addition to its historic lighthouses. offers camping and picnicking facilities as well as trails for hiking and skiing. For more information visit mnhs.org/splitrock or call (218) 226–6372.

Many believe the Split Rock Lighthouse (opposite page) is the most scenic building on the Great Lakes. For more than half a century, however, sailors on Lake Superior looked to the tower for guidance rather than beauty.

THOMAS P. SHEARER/MOMENT VIA GETTY IMAGES

Part Six

ROMANTIC BEACONS OF THE IMPERIAL COAST

Canada

Since they serve all ships and sailors without regard to nationality, lighthouses are a country's best ambassadors. This is particularly true of lighthouses on the Great Lakes, where they not only make navigation easier and safer but also provide a highly visible link of friendship between the United States and Canada.

Together with the St. Lawrence River, the Great Lakes form one of the most extensive watery borders in the world—and one of the most peaceful. The United States and Canada have not taken up arms against one another in more than 180 years. This friendly relationship between the two nations is due partly to a common heritage but also to the need for efficient management of the lakes as a natural resource and commercial thoroughfare.

In almost every sense, the United States and Canada share the Great Lakes. The St. Lawrence Seaway, which opened the interior of the continent to oceangoing freighters and enriched both countries, was a joint venture. To reach the bustling freshwater ports of Toronto, Cleveland, Detroit, Chicago, and Thunder Bay, ships moving up the seaway from the Atlantic must pass into and out of American and Canadian jurisdiction many times. The crews of these ships are often unsure whether they are in US or Canadian waters. The Welland Canal is Canadian, the Soo Locks, American and Canadian.

Only Michigan is an all-American lake, and Canadian vessels ply its waters every day during the shipping season. In other words, instead of separating the two countries, the lakes help bring them together.

The international quality of the lakes comes into clearest focus when their restless waters turn violent. The captain of a freighter caught in a storm on the lakes does not care whether his ship is on the Canadian or American side—only that it remains afloat. The crew of a foundering vessel is equally joyous at the sight of either a Canadian Coast Guard or U.S. Coast Guard cutter. Shipwrecked sailors don't much care about the nationality of their rescuers.

To help keep wrecks to a minimum and guide vessels safely to their destinations, a continuous line of lighthouses marks both sides of the seaway, from the mouth of the St. Lawrence River all the way to the far end of Lake Superior, a shoreline distance of more than 1,000 miles. Those lighthouses on the Canadian side are in every way as varied, historical, and beautiful as their counterparts on the opposite shores. This chapter offers a sampling of some of the finest Canadian lighthouses on the Great Lakes.

Nine Mile Point Light
Simcoe Island, Ontario
1834

The Nine Mile Point Lighthouse was the first link in a chain of lights stretching hundreds of miles from Kingston, at the eastern end of Lake Ontario, to Thunder Bay, near the far end of Lake Superior. This light once was thought to be of vital strategic importance. The government of Upper Canada considered construction of a lighthouse here a priority, and in 1833 it provided 750 pounds sterling ($2,918) for the purpose. But these were far more frugal times than our own, and apparently not all this money was spent.

A patriotic island property owner donated land for the station on the condition that the government "put up a good fence." The station's iron lantern was purchased for 139 pounds ($542), while another 172 pounds ($670) went to provide lamps, reflectors, oil burners, and other supplies. Construction of the tower—often the most expensive single consideration when establishing a light station—cost about 317 pounds ($1,236). The 45-foot stone structure, built by one Robert Mathews, proved to have been worth every shilling. The station's beacon is no longer active, but the tower still stands today despite more than one and a half centuries of buffeting by storm-driven winds whistling off the lake.

How to Get There

A visit to Nine Mile Point Lighthouse requires two ferry rides, one from the charming town of Kingston to Wolfe Island and another to nearby Simcoe Island. While the adventure of getting there may be worth the trouble, the lighthouse is closed to the public and must be viewed from a fence some distance from the tower. Once back in Kingston, visitors should explore the excellent Marine Museum of the Great Lakes located on the waterfront. For more information check the museum website at marmuseum.ca.

Nine Mile Point Lighthouse marks Ontario's Simcoe Island, strategically located near the entrance of the St. Lawrence River. Its red-and-white colors are typical of Canadian lighthouses. SCOTT SHYMKO/MOMENT VIA GETTY IMAGES

Lights of Prince Edward County

False Duck Island Light (1829), Prince Edward Point Light (1881), Main Duck Island Light (1913)

At one time or another, at least twelve separate light stations have guarded Prince Edward County's shores: the lighthouses at False Duck Island (built in 1829), Point Petre (1833), Presqu'ile Point (1854), Scotch Bonnet Reef (1856), Point Pleasant (1866), Telegraph Island (1870), Salmon Point (1871), Point Traverse (1881), Prince Edward Point (1881), Makatewis Island (1894), Onderdonk Point (1911), and Main Duck Island (1913). But time has been as hard on these old lighthouses as the county itself has been on ships. All but a few of the lighthouses have been abandoned, and most have fallen into ruins or disappeared altogether.

The oldest lighthouse in the county stood for many years on False Duck Island, which was often mistaken by ships' pilots for Main Duck Island. Built of concrete and stone at a cost of approximately 1,000 British pounds ($3,890), the station featured a 63-foot tower displaying a fixed white light provided by oil lamps.

One night in 1905 an extraordinarily powerful trident of lightning struck the station, blasting apart the lantern room and burning the dwelling and oil house to the ground.

The station was fully restored and served until 1965, when the venerable lighthouse was replaced by an automated navigational marker. That same year a Canadian Coast Guard tender hooked a cable to the historic tower and pulled it to the ground, thus accomplishing what lightning had not: the utter destruction of a national treasure.

Only a few miles from the park stands the decaying remains of Prince Edward Point Lighthouse. Built in 1881, it guided mariners for almost 80 years before finally giving up its job to a fully automated light atop a nearby steel-skeleton tower. When it was decommissioned in 1959, the old lighthouse suffered the indignity of having its lantern removed, and it has been more or less neglected ever since. Indeed, nowadays paint peels from the tapered wooden walls of the decapitated tower.

Not all of the county's light stations serve only as memorials, however. After more than 80 years of nightly vigilance, the Main Duck Island Lighthouse still flashes its warning to ships every six seconds. Established shortly before World War I, the station marks the western end of Main Duck Island, a 15-mile-long barrier of ship-killing rock more than a dozen miles from the Ontario mainland. The 70-foot octagonal tower contains a rotating, third-order Fresnel lens, producing an intermittent beam visible from 16 miles away.

How to Get There

Mariner's Memorial Park can be reached from the town of Picton via county roads off Highway 33. The park museum features excellent nautical exhibits and a fine collection of old-time sailing artifacts. For more information on the museum and Prince Edward County lighthouses visit peilighthousesociety.org or thecounty.ca museum pages.

Gibraltar Point Light
Toronto, Ontario
1806

The Gibraltar Point Lighthouse has saved hundreds, perhaps thousands, of vessels by guiding them to safety. A lighthouse does its most effective lifesaving work when a disaster does not occur. Who can say how many wrecks there might have been if not for the tall octagonal tower on Gibraltar Point? One of the earliest navigational markers on the Great Lakes, the lighthouse was built in 1806 on the lakeward crook of a low, sandy island shaped like a fishhook. The brown-brick tower served mariners for more than 150 years before being replaced by a fully automated light mounted on a simple iron tower in 1958.

Among the most historic navigational markers in Canada, or anywhere, the two-century-old Gibraltar Point Lighthouse is said to be haunted by the ghost of its first keeper. M-KOJOT/ISTOCK VIA GETTY IMAGES

Gibraltar Point is said to be haunted. The very first keeper of the lighthouse here was a man named Rademuller. In 1815 Rademuller vanished from the island and was never seen or heard from again. Some years later, however, his skeleton was unearthed near the tower, making it apparent that the hapless keeper had been murdered. His ghost is said to walk the island and to climb the lighthouse steps at night.

How to Get There
The Gibraltar Point Lighthouse can be reached by taking the Harlan Point Ferry from the terminal just off Queen's Quay and Young Street on the Toronto waterfront. The Queen's Wharf Lighthouse is located off Fleet Street, not far from Exhibition Stadium. For more information on Toronto Island Park, and other fascinating Toronto destinations visit Torontoisland.com or Toronto.ca.

Port Burwell Light
Port Burwell, Ontario
1840

One of the most beautiful wooden structures in all Canada, the classic octagonal tower of the Port Burwell Lighthouse has stood since 1840. The tower's gently sloping walls are 65 feet high and crested by a small, eight-sided lantern room containing a fourth-order Fresnel lens.

The Canadian Coast Guard decommissioned the light in 1963, after 123 years of service. Astonishingly, for all but the first twelve of those years, the lighthouse was looked after by members of the same family. Alexander Sutherland became keeper in 1852. He was succeeded in the post by his sons and grandsons right up until the light was finally extinguished, a family service record of 111 years in all.

Although the lighthouse no longer guides ships, a ceremonial light still burns atop the tower. The old lighthouse is carefully maintained by citizens of Port Burwell, who consider it a vital link to their past. Using traditional hand tools, Mennonite craftsmen completed renovations in 1986. Near the lighthouse is the Port Burwell Marine Museum, which contains a fine collection of lighthouse and maritime artifacts. Especially noteworthy among the displays is the three-sided bull's-eye lens and rotation drive that once served at the nearby Old Long Point Lighthouse.

How to Get There
Port Burwell can be reached from Highway 3 via Highway 19, which ends at Robinson Street near the lighthouse and adjacent maritime museum. For more information visit bayham.on.ca or call (519) 874–4807.

Lights of Manitoulin Island

Mississagi Straits Light
1873

Janet Head (Gore Bay) Light (1879), Kagawong Light (1880), South Baymouth Front Range Light (1898)

Built in 1873, the oldest surviving lighthouse on Manitoulin Island still maintains its vigil beside the crucial Mississagi Straits. The light, mounted atop a square, 40-foot wooden tower, once guided ships passing between the broad North Channel and Lake Huron. Although the lighthouse was taken out of service in 1970, a nearby automated light continues its vitally important work.

The tower rises from a corner of a modest dwelling where keepers once lived with their families. For these keepers, the Mississagi Straits Lighthouse was a particularly isolated duty station. The only way in or out was over a rugged trail or by boat; not until 1968, when the light was about to be automated, did construction crews push through a road to the station. Nevertheless, the longevity of service for keepers at this station was remarkable. During almost a century of operation, only five keepers served here. W. A. Grant kept the light for almost 33 years, living at this remote out-post with his wife and family from 1913 until 1946. A local historical society operates a museum here during the summer and has filled the dwelling with authentic period furnishings. It is easy to imagine that any of the station's keepers could step into the dwelling and feel right at home.

Very similar to the Mississagi Straits Lighthouse is the 25-foot tower and attached dwelling at Janet Head. During the 1820s a British naval officer named this headland for his daughter. Built in 1879, the Janet Head Lighthouse was retired in 1940. This station also had five different keepers, the longest term of service being that of Robert Lewis, who kept the light from 1913 until 1932.

To mark the harbor of the industrious village of Kagawong, the Canadian govern-ment established a light on Mudge Bay in 1880. It shined from a small tower built out over the water at the end of a dock. A fire, probably sparked by the coal-oil lamps in the lantern room, soon destroyed the tower, and it was replaced by a small pyramidal structure built on shore. Completed in 1888, Kagawong's second lighthouse survives to this day. The 30-foot wooden tower supports a square lantern room displaying a red light visible from 13 miles away.

After an earlier Kagawong tower was destroyed by fire, it was replaced in 1888 by this pyramidal wooden structure which still stands and guides vessels to this day.

A slightly taller pyramidal tower still marks the western shore of Manitowaning Bay, just as it has since 1885. The 35-foot-tall lighthouse stands on a hill in the village of Manitowaning. Beaming from an octagonal lantern room, its green light can be seen from a distance of up to 16 miles.

At South Baymouth, near the entrance to whale-shaped South Bay, a Tweedledee–Tweedledum range lighthouse combination teams up to mark the safe channel for vessels approaching the town. Built in 1898, the white wooden towers stand about 250 yards apart; they are so similar in appearance that looking at them in the daylight makes you wonder if you are seeing double. The structures are not identical, however. The 26-foot rear tower is taller and thinner than its 17-foot mate located down near the water. It is the perspective that makes them look the same.

How to Get There

Because of the island's enormous size, visitors should set aside ample time, perhaps a week or more, to properly see and enjoy the many Manitoulin Island lighthouses and other attractions. The island can be reached from the Canadian mainland by crossing the Great LaCloche Island Bridge on Highway 6, which leads to the town of Mani-towaning, with its beautiful and historic lighthouse. Highway 6 eventually dead-ends at South Baymouth, which features a pair of pyramidal wooden range light towers near its busy ferry terminal. Lighthouses to the north and west of Highway 6 can be accessed via secondary roads off Highways 540 or 542. These include the Kagawong Lighthouse to the north of the town of Kagawong, Janet Head Lighthouse north of Gore Bay, and the Mississagi Strait Lighthouse west of Meldrum Bay. A detailed road map and GPS are highly recommended. For more information visit destinationmanito-ulinisland.com or call (705) 368–3021.

Lights of the Bruce Peninsula

Travelers headed toward Bruce Peninsula along the shore of Lake Huron will likely pass through the town of Goderich and very near one of Ontario's oldest lighthouses. On a bluff above the lake, just a few blocks off Canada's scenic Highway 21, a squar-ish concrete tower guards the approaches to Goderich Harbor. Only 35 feet tall, the Goderich Main Lighthouse is rather quaint compared to the Imperial Towers at Point Clark and Chantry Island to the north (see Imperial Towers, beginning on page 115). This workmanlike lighthouse does its job well, however, guiding vessels into and out of the harbor, just as it has done since 1847.

Goderich Main Light
1847

Marking the approaches to one of the loveliest towns in Canada, the Goderich Main Lighthouse dates to 1847. It is shown here flying the flags of Canada and the Canadian Coast Guard.

Kincardine Rear Range Light
1888

In Kincardine, about 40 miles to the north of Goderich, stands a lighthouse that nearly everyone considers beautiful. The unique design and picture-postcard good looks of the Kincardine Rear Range Lighthouse are a boon for businesses in this delightful lakeshore community. The octagonal wooden tower rises gracefully some 30 feet above the roof of the dwelling. Both the tower and dwelling are painted white with red trim. Built in 1888, the lighthouse is one of two working in tandem to guide vessels into the harbor. Located on a wharf about a quarter of a mile away, the small Kincardine Front Range tower is much less remarkable.

MARCPO/ISTOCK VIA GETTY IMAGES

Cape Crocker Light
1898

Marking the northern shore of rectangular Colpoy's Bay, which forms a 10-mile-long slot on the east side of the Bruce Peninsula, is the Cape Crocker Lighthouse (the Imperial Tower on Griffith Island marks the southern shore). The lantern of the Cape Crocker Light is similar in style to those atop the magnificent Imperials, but the tower itself could hardly be more different. Its smooth octagonal walls are no wider than the lantern and convey the impression of a pole or pedestal. A fanciful mind might see the 53-foot-tall structure as a torch designed to be carried by a giant runner—and what a torch it would be. The lantern contains a powerful, third-order Fresnel clamshell lens displaying a flashing green light.

Cabot Head Light
1896

The Cabot Head Lighthouse, perhaps the homiest light station on the Bruce Peninsula, appears ready for a keeper's family to move right in and live in the traditional style. The station dates to 1896. Looked after nowadays by the Friends of Cabot Head, the

MARCPO/ISTOCK VIA GETTY IMAGES

dwelling has been furnished with antiques and decorated in a manner reminiscent of earlier times. The group hopes to restore the tower that once rose from a corner of the dwelling. The top of the tower was lopped off several years ago when a nearby airport-style beacon went into service.

How to Get There

Much of the scenic and tourist-friendly Bruce Peninsula is traversed by Highway 6 which runs all the way to the end of its 100-mile-long northward thumb. Several beautiful lighthouses can be reached via secondary roads leading either to the east or west of the highway (A detailed road map and GPS are highly recommended). To reach the Cape Crocker Lighthouse, visitors travel northwest of the town of Wiarton on County Roads 9 and 18 before taking the long and windy access road leading to Cape Crocker Park The Cabot Head Lighthouse is to the east of the highway near the village of Dyer's Bay and can be reached via a five-mile-long access road. For more information on the scenic wonders of the Bruce Peninsula including its lighthouses go to visitbrucepeninsula.ca or thebrucepeninsula.com. Parts of the peninsula are included in the popular Bruce Peninsula National Park. For more information on the park visit the Parks Canada website at pc.gc.ca.

Several notable lighthouses mark the long, westward-facing base of the peninsula. Among these is the Goderich Main Lighthouse to the west of Highway 21 in Goderich, Ontario. Its squared-off tower is the primary attraction of Lighthouse Park near the end of Lighthouse Avenue. The popular and scenic St. Cristopher's Beach extends along the nearby lakefront. For more information visit Goderich.ca. About 40 miles north of Goderich is the quaint town of Kincardine where the eight-sided wooden tower of the Kincardine Rear Range Lighthouse graces the banks of the Penetagore River. Located below Harbour Street to the west of Highway 21, the light tower and adjacent buildings house a maritime museum open during the summer. More information is available at visitkinkardine.com.

The Imperial Towers

Nottawasaga Island Light (1858), Cove Island Light (1859), Chantry Island Light (1859), Point Clark Light (1859)

During the nineteenth century, lake sailors considered the Bruce Peninsula a death trap for ships, its wild and rugged shoreline threatening always to tear apart the hulls of wayward vessels. Recognizing the dangers that this knife-shaped peninsula posed to shipping, the Canadian government hired Ontario contractor John Brown to build a series of lighthouses marking prominent points and warning sailors away from ship-killing shoals.

Among the first of the tall towers built by John Brown was the crucial Cove Island Lighthouse, which marks the Main Channel connecting Lake Huron to Georgian Bay. Work on the station apparently began as early as 1856 (the year is scratched into concrete inside the tower), and its light first guided sailors in 1859. Against a lushly forested background, the whitewashed stone tower rises more than 85 feet above the lake. At the top a red lantern room, encircled by a polygon of square windowpanes, houses a powerful, second-order Fresnel lens.

Vessels approaching Collingwood Harbor have often come to grief on the shoals and ledges that make the southern tip of Nottawasaga Bay a sailor's nightmare. To warn ships of the danger, Brown built the tallest of his towers here, on rugged Nottawasaga Island. The 95-foot tower was ready for service in 1858. But the need for a light was so great that keepers hung a makeshift lantern from the unfinished tower each night until the work was complete and the official lighting apparatus in place. The light was automated in 1959, almost exactly 101 years after it went into service. It still does its job, but nowadays it does so without the help of a keeper.

Located on Chantry Island, near the far southwestern hip of the Bruce Peninsula, another of Brown's stone lighthouses still does the work it was built for in 1859. Warning ships away from the island and the rocky coastline beyond, the 86-foot tower looks much like the other Imperials. Its light was automated in 1954.

About 60 miles south of the peninsula, the stubby thumb of Point Clark juts out into Lake Huron, pointing toward a shoal only two miles offshore. To warn ships of this dangerous obstacle, Brown's workmen built the last and, perhaps, the most spectacular of the Imperial Towers. Completed in 1859, the tower soars 87 feet above the relatively flat headland. The Point Clark Lighthouse was declared a National Historic Site in 1967.

How to Get There

The magnificent Point Clark Lighthouse, located off Highway 21 a few miles south of Kincardine, is easily accessible by road. However, the other Imperial Towers are more remote. In most cases, the best way to see them is by private boat or from the deck of a ferry. For more information visit ontarioferries.ca or the Parks Canada website at pc.gc.ca.

Index

Presque Isle Light, 27, 44
Prince Edward Point Light, 104

R
Raspberry Island Light, 90
Rawley Point Light, 67

S
Sand Island Light, 92
Selkirk (Port Ontario) Light, 14
Seul Choix Point Light, 73
Sodus Point Lighthouse, 15
South Baymouth Front Range Light, 107
Split Rock Lighthouse, 97
Sturgeon Point Light, 41

T
Tawas Point Light, 40
Thirty Mile Point Light, 17
Tibbetts Point Light, 13
Toledo Harbor Light, 31
Two Harbors Light, 96

W
Whitefish Point Light, 80
Wind Point Light, 65

About the Author

Ray Jones is a writer and publishing consultant living in Pebble Beach, California. Author of more than fifty books, Ray began his writing career as a reporter for weekly newspapers in Texas. He has served as a senior editor and writing coach at *Southern Living* magazine, an editor for Time-Life Books, founding editor of *Albuquerque Living* magazine, and founder and publisher of Country Roads Press. Ray grew up in Macon, Georgia, where he was inspired by the writing of Ernest Hemingway and William Faulkner, and worked his way through college as a disc jockey.